Cambridge Student Guide

Shakespeare

Julius Caesar

Anthony Davies

Series Editor: Rex Gibson

CAMBRIDGE
UNIVERSITY PRESS

PUBLISHED BY THE PRESS SYNDICATE OF THE UNIVERSITY OF CAMBRIDGE
The Pitt Building, Trumpington Street, Cambridge, United Kingdom

CAMBRIDGE UNIVERSITY PRESS
The Edinburgh Building, Cambridge CB2 2RU, UK
40 West 20th Street, New York, NY 10011–4211, USA
477 Williamstown Road, Port Melbourne, VIC 3207, Australia
Ruiz de Alarcón 13, 28014 Madrid, Spain
Dock House, The Waterfront, Cape Town 8001, South Africa

http://www.cambridge.org

First published 2002

Printed in the United Kingdom at the University Press, Cambridge

Typeface 9.5/12pt Scala   *System* QuarkXPress®

A catalogue record for this book is available from the British Library

ISBN 0 521 00823 9 paperback

Contents

Introduction

Ever since it was first performed in 1599, *Julius Caesar* has proved immensely popular with audiences. The scholar Steve Sohmer claims that Shakespeare's *Julius Caesar* 'has run through more editions, and more copies, than any play in any language'.

Why has the play held such fascinating appeal for over 400 years? In spite of the many words written about it, and all its performances, Shakespeare's *Julius Caesar* suggests that little has changed in the way political power is sought after by some and resented or suspected by others. Just as in Shakespeare's play Brutus and Antony rely on the rhetorical devices of language to justify their actions to those whom they need to persuade, so do modern politicians.

The seemingly simple question, 'What is the play about?' yields a host of answers. One might be that the play is about the murder of a man who has become too powerful. Another view might regard Brutus as the central character, and so the play could become the tragedy of Brutus. Perhaps it could be explained as the interaction of four very different characters – Caesar, Antony, Brutus and Cassius – whose changing relationships both shape – and are shaped by – the assassination of Caesar, a study in friendship and betrayal. Other responses might interpret it as a play about the incompatibility of political ideals with political practicalities, or a play about body and spirit.

The play continually reflects Shakespeare's sense of theatre. The dramatic action constantly involves individual characters speaking and performing to other individuals or to gatherings. The stabbing of Caesar is a public event. Cassius wonders how often future generations will re-enact 'our lofty scene'. Brutus and Antony stand on platforms and become actors as well as orators. Modern productions often unite the theatre audience with the plebeians so that Brutus and Antony address the two audiences as one.

This theatricality and its continuing relevance to the politics of the modern world contribute significantly to *Julius Caesar*'s capacity for being interpreted afresh. This Guide will help you to see that although the play is deeply rooted in the preoccupations of Elizabethan England, it remains sharply relevant in its dramatisation of power and authority.

Commentary

Act 1 Scene 1

'Hence! Home, you idle creatures, get you home!' Flavius' words which open the play make it clear that he and his fellow tribune, Murellus, do not share the enjoyment of the plebeians, the ordinary people of Rome. The crowd is in a carnival mood, waiting to welcome Julius Caesar home after his triumphant victory in the civil war that shook the political stability of Rome. The two tribunes clearly resent the downfall of Pompey, whom Caesar defeated. They are stung to anger by the festive behaviour they now witness.

Far from changing the buoyant mood of the crowd, Flavius and Murellus find themselves mocked, especially by the cobbler, who outwits Flavius with his punning on 'soles'/souls, being 'out' and 'all'/'awl'. The cobbler will not speak again in the play, but he is dramatically important for two reasons. First, he shows that language and the way it is used will be a major concern of the play. Second, it is he who first speaks the name of the character around whom the action of the play will revolve: Caesar.

Murellus uses more subtle verbal tactics than Flavius. Before he orders the crowd to go home, he puts a well-developed argument to them. He reminds the plebeians that they had once been just as enthusiastic about Pompey's passing through Rome as they now are about Caesar. He asks eight questions, at moments crowding them together to intensify their force:

> And do you now put on your best attire?
> And do you now cull out a holiday?
> And do you now strew flowers in his way,
> That comes in triumph over Pompey's blood?   *(lines 47–50)*

Unlike Flavius' earlier questions, these do not seek answers from the people he is addressing. They are rhetorical questions, intended to redirect the thinking of his listeners, to persuade them to examine their actions. Flavius' disapproval had focused audience attention on his quick exchange of comment with the crowd. Murellus' long speech now requires a director to focus attention on him and to place him prominently on stage. Murellus is a skilled orator. He has learned the rules of rhetoric, the language techniques that can persuade an audience. His speech foreshadows the persuasive oratory that will recur at many points as the play develops.

There is a shape and form to Murellus' 24 lines. After his initial questions, he is momentarily aggressively critical of the crowd. He reduces them to unfeeling objects: 'You blocks, you stones, you worse than senseless things!' But he immediately restores their humanity, appealing to them as men: 'O you hard hearts, you cruel men of Rome, / Knew you not Pompey?'

Using another technique of the crafty orator, he piles up item on item to remind them of Rome and what it means to be a Roman. Their military tradition is recalled in his mention of Rome's 'walls', its 'battlements' and 'towers'. The domestic life of the city is evoked with 'windows', 'chimney tops' and 'Your infants in your arms'. To these he adds another feature with which all Romans would be familiar – the River Tiber, which

> trembled underneath her banks
> To hear the replication of your sounds
> Made in her concave shores?   *(lines 44–6)*

Murellus reminds them of how they responded with excitement, climbing to high points to wait 'To see great Pompey pass the streets of Rome.'

From 'blocks' and 'stones', Murellus has cleverly implied that the plebeians are men. Even more cunningly, he has acknowledged them as citizens of Rome, with the special richness of heritage that being a Roman carries with it.

A stage director has to decide what response is appropriate from the crowd to Murellus' speech. Has he subdued them in shame, or do they leave muttering with resentment? Is their resentment more angrily expressed, perhaps with gestures of defiance? The only suggestion of their mood as they leave comes from Flavius, who suggests that 'their basest metal' is 'moved', and that 'They vanish tongue-tied in their guiltiness.' But Flavius might be interpreting the crowd's departure as he would like to see it. As politicians usually do, perhaps he is putting a spin on an event.

When the two tribunes are alone onstage, Flavius decides that they should set about removing the decorations from Caesar's statues. He ends the scene with a clear comment on Caesar's rise to power, and a determination to check his dangerous ambition to rule Rome as a dictator:

> These growing feathers plucked from Caesar's wing
> Will make him fly an ordinary pitch,
> Who else would soar above the view of men
> And keep us all in servile fearfulness.   *(lines 71–4)*

This is the only appearance of Murellus and Flavius in the play, but they emerge as interestingly different personalities. Both are unhappy about the rising importance of Caesar. Murellus sees Caesar's recently won popularity as evidence of the plebeians' disloyalty to Pompey. Flavius seems moved more by personal animosity, and wishes to destroy any signs of Caesar's growing power and influence.

Scene 1 opens up three issues. The first concerns the plebeians. Before the play opens they had excitedly cheered Pompey as he passed through the city streets. Now they enthusiastically celebrate Caesar's return to Rome. The question of their loyalty will reverberate through the play: do they switch their allegiance all too easily from one leader to another? The second issue concerns the tribunes. How differently do the leaders of Rome behave in public compared to when they are alone together? The difference between what might be called 'public and private appearance' is evident in the scene, and will recur through the play. The third element in the scene concerns motivation. Although men may be united in action (opposing Caesar), their individual motives may be very different.

Act 1 Scene 2

Typically, Shakespeare has prepared for the entrance of the play's main character by having relatively unimportant characters talk about him in the opening scene. Now Caesar enters to preside over the games of Lupercal. But Caesar's first word in the play seems surprising; it is his wife's name, 'Calpurnia'. Coming straight after Flavius' bitter assessment that Caesar wishes to 'keep us all in servile fearfulness' it refers not to Caesar's political ambitions, but to his private life. Despite the very public setting of the scene, it is Caesar the vulnerable human being who is revealed as he makes clear his unhappiness at having no child by his wife. When he asks Antony to touch Calpurnia as he runs past her in the games, he clutches at the superstition that such a ritual action might cure infertility:

> The barren, touchèd in this holy chase,
> Shake off their sterile curse. *(lines 8–9)*

Caesar's progress is interrupted by the urgent shout of the Soothsayer who warns him to 'Beware the Ides of March'. Ironically it is Brutus – who will play a major part in the conspiracy – who repeats the warning to Caesar. Caesar's response perhaps provides a further clue to his character. Why is he so intent on hearing what the Soothsayer says, only to dismiss him as a dreamer? Caesar's instincts, it seems, persuade him to listen closely to the Soothsayer's ominous words, while his awareness of the many eyes upon him prompts him to show that he is unperturbed by the warning. He cannot be seen to fear danger.

With Caesar's exit the focus of the scene shifts to Cassius and Brutus. The shouts and applause of the crowd will still occasionally intrude, but the conversation between the two men is sustained and intimate. There is a hint of reproach in Cassius' opening lines. He reminds Brutus of their friendship, but says he has recently noticed an unusual remoteness. Brutus admits that his mind has been troubled by other matters, and so he has neglected his courtesy to his friends.

Cassius now begins to reveal what is in his own mind. He asks Brutus if he can see his own face. Brutus replies that one can only see oneself 'by reflection'. This opens the way for Cassius to speak of what really concerns him. He reveals that many influential Romans have suggested to him that Brutus appears blind to the harshness of 'this age's yoke': the tyranny of the times. Significantly, Cassius excludes Caesar from those influential Romans, referring to him (probably sarcastically) as 'immortal Caesar'. Brutus quickly senses a danger in Cassius' line of thought:

> Into what dangers would you lead me, Cassius,
> That you would have me seek into myself
> For that which is not in me? *(lines 63–5)*

Brutus' response is ambiguous. By 'that which is not in me' does he mean the noble qualities Cassius has described as 'hidden worthiness', or does he already suspect that Cassius is urging him to question the friendship and dutiful support he has developed for Caesar?

The shouting of the distant crowd in the arena interrupts the conversation and Brutus' reaction gives a clue to his thoughts. He is prompted to 'fear [that] the people / Choose Caesar for their king'. His fear provides Cassius with an opportunity. He has perceived a conflict in Brutus' mind between his Republican idealism and his loyalty to Caesar. Brutus is clearly opposed to Caesar's becoming the sole ruler of Rome. Whatever it is that Cassius wants of him, he will do, if it is for the general good of Rome, for that would be honourable.

Cassius seizes on Brutus' concern for 'honour'. He clearly wishes to persuade Brutus that if Caesar becomes king he will be a dictator and a danger to Rome. To reveal the ordinary human frailty of this Caesar, whom people are treating like a god, Cassius gives two accounts as evidence of Caesar's weakness. He recalls the time he rescued Caesar from the water in a swimming contest, and Caesar's cry for water 'As a sick girl' when he was ill with a fever in Spain.

Cassius' purpose is to show that to submit without question to Caesar, who is merely a man like all other men, is both demeaning and, in itself, dishonourable. Just how Brutus might respond to Cassius' bitter memories will depend on how an actor might convey the character's feeling through movement and gesture. Shakespeare aids the actor in taking such decisions with yet another offstage shout from the crowd in the stadium. Brutus fears that further 'new honours' are being 'heaped on Caesar'. Brutus' disquiet at the popular acclaim for Caesar prompts Cassius to make his intentions quite evident:

> Why, man, he doth bestride the narrow world
> Like a Colossus, and we petty men
> Walk under his huge legs and peep about
> To find ourselves dishonourable graves.   *(lines 135–8)*

Cassius shifts from the intimacy of conversation to the style of an orator, employing the rhetorical techniques that will feature so strongly throughout the play. He seems to hold a name like an object in each hand, as he compares them. 'Brutus and Caesar: what should be in that "Caesar"?' He juggles with them, making Caesar's name ordinary and loading Brutus' with significance. That significance will be clear to Brutus, and was familiar to many in Shakespeare's audience; he reminds Brutus of the illustrious past and of his ancestor, another Brutus who drove the Tarquin kings from Rome and founded the 400-year-old Republic. Using all his persuasive skill, Cassius is intent on rousing Brutus to act to prevent Rome being ruled by 'but one only man': Caesar.

Cassius' tactics succeed. Brutus says he understands what Cassius wants him to do. He resolves to consider it, but to give his decision later. His response reveals important aspects of his character: he is not one to be carried lightly on the current of another's plans, and he resists Cassius' pressure to commit himself on impulse. But his final words clearly indicate his determination to resist the prospect of the tyranny that seems likely if Caesar becomes king:

> Till then, my noble friend, chew upon this:
> Brutus had rather be a villager
> Than to repute himself a son of Rome
> Under these hard conditions as this time
> Is like to lay upon us. *(lines 171–5)*

Caesar's retinue returns from the games and Brutus remarks on the dejected mood of Caesar's party, the anger of his expression, the pallor of Calpurnia, and the 'fiery eyes' of Cicero.

Caesar confides to Antony his distrust of Cassius. In their different ways, both Caesar and Cassius are astute judges of character. But Antony, whom Caesar trusts, seems surprisingly naive, assuring Caesar that Cassius is 'a noble Roman and well given'. Caesar's description of Cassius is that of the typical Elizabethan malcontent, a theatrical character who comments with caustic bitterness on society and is often bent on revenge. It is significant that Caesar insists twice that he does not personally fear Cassius, but he recognises in him 'what is to be feared'. Perhaps Antony's earlier 'Fear him not, Caesar' touched a sensitive nerve. In ironic contrast to all the earlier comment on Caesar as a god, Shakespeare presents him as a man afflicted with certain physical weaknesses. Caesar's parting admission that he is deaf in his left ear is a further indication of his human frailty.

With the exit of Caesar and his attendants the stage is left to Cassius, Brutus and Casca. Cassius and Brutus set about drawing Casca out on the happenings in the games arena. Casca's lengthy responses, delivered more as a light commentary on the entire occasion, contrast with the seriousness of Brutus and Cassius, and bring a new dramatic dimension onto the stage.

Casca's report suggests what probably made Caesar angry. Perhaps it was the difficult position he found himself in, being offered a symbolic crown and having to refuse it in public. Casca says that Caesar was offered 'one of these coronets' three times, and that on each occasion, as he 'put it by' (refused it), there was loud applause from the 'rabblement'. Was he being tested by the mass of spectators? Was there a conflict between Caesar's private desire to be crowned and his awareness of the popular distaste for a monarchy?

Clearly no lover of crowds and mass emotion, Casca's contempt for the common people comes through very clearly. His descriptions are entertaining, but they raise again the question of the fickleness of the Roman plebeians:

> Three or four wenches where I stood cried, 'Alas, good soul', and forgave him with all their hearts. But there's no heed to be taken of them: if Caesar had stabbed their mothers they would have done no less. *(lines 262–5)*

Casca's report of Caesar's fainting and falling down (epilepsy) is another suggestion of his physical frailty. Cassius, as if to invite Casca to speak more openly, says it is not Caesar, but Casca, himself and Brutus who have 'the falling sickness'. Casca claims he does not understand Cassius' meaning, but perhaps he senses a trap in Cassius' comment. It is dangerous to be openly critical of Caesar. That danger is made evident as Casca reports the execution of the two tribunes:

> Murellus and Flavius, for pulling scarves off Caesar's images, are put to silence. *(lines 274–5)*

In the closing 15 lines of the scene, Cassius is left alone on stage. His soliloquy reveals his true thoughts. He acknowledges Brutus' nobility of nature, but detects that his honourable qualities may be turned from noble purposes. Cassius proposes using this flaw in Brutus' nature to corrupt him to join the plot against Caesar.

He resolves to throw through Brutus' window a number of letters, written as though from several respectable citizens. All will reassure him of 'the great opinion / That Rome holds of his name' and each will hint at the danger of Caesar's ambition. The concluding couplet of the scene makes clear how important Brutus' support will be for the conspiracy that will topple Caesar:

> And after this let Caesar seat him sure,
> For we will shake him, or worse days endure.   *(lines 310–11)*

Act 1 Scene 3

The mood of this scene contrasts strongly with what has gone before. An awareness of crowds and daylight was central to the play's action in the first two scenes. Here, the action takes place between a few individuals at night, and the stage directions call for 'Thunder and lightning'. Bearing in mind that in Shakespeare's day plays were staged in daylight and the theatre was unable to produce spectacular lighting effects, it is interesting to speculate on how the storm effects might have been produced at The Globe in 1599. An Elizabethan audience would have understood the theatrical conventions of the time and would, no doubt, have responded fully to the sustained images of the storm that recur in the descriptions of both Casca and Cassius.

In this theatrical creation of storm and darkness, entering from opposite sides of the stage, Casca and Cicero meet. In line with theatrical convention, the language of Casca's opening question to Cicero, 'Are not you moved when all the sway of earth / Shakes like a thing unfirm?' is perhaps as important for creating the atmosphere of the scene as for revealing Casca's agitation.

From the brief mention in Scene 2, Cicero appears politically astute, being careful to speak in Greek when he makes comments on Caesar at the games of Lupercal. Cicero was in fact a famous orator and a scholar. He produced eloquent Latin versions of the writings of the Greek philosophers. For him, the storm seems to mean nothing extraordinary. Indeed, he reacts with more surprise to Casca's alarm than to the storm's power.

Casca seems a changed man. In Scene 2 he appeared to be an

urbane, composed and witty commentator on events. Now he reveals a very different side of his character. For him, this storm is unlike anything he has seen before and is filled with frightening omens. It is 'a tempest dropping fire', which he takes to mean either that the gods are fighting with each other or that they wish to destroy the world. Casca goes on to recall in detail what has disturbed him: a familiar slave holding up his burning hand, a lion which stared at him and 'went surly by', ghostly women who claimed they saw flaming men walking in the streets, and an owl which hooted in the market place at midday.

Casca's report gives insight into Shakespeare's working methods as a dramatist. In Plutarch, the Greek historian on whose writings Shakespeare drew (see page 65), we read:

> There was a slave of the soldiers that did cast a marvellous
> burning flame out of his hand, inasmuch as they that saw it
> thought he had been burnt, but when the fire was out, it was
> found he had no hurt.

Shakespeare's dramatic imagination transforms Plutarch's description into a vivid image:

> A common slave – you know him well by sight –
> Held up his left hand, which did flame and burn
> Like twenty torches joined, and yet his hand,
> Not sensible of fire, remained unscorched.   *(lines 15–18)*

Casca ends his account convinced of the significance of what he has seen. Events in the natural world seem to portend great changes for Rome:

> For I believe they are portentous things
> Unto the climate that they point upon.   *(lines 31–2)*

Cicero's response is ambiguous. On one level, his 'Indeed, it is a strange-disposèd time' might refer to the storm itself. On another, he might be referring to the gathering political disaffection in Rome. Like the astute politician he is, he holds back from offering any clear opinion:

> But men may construe things after their fashion
> Clean from the purpose of the things themselves. *(lines 34–5)*

Cicero then asks Casca if Caesar intends coming to the Capitol on the next day. Here Shakespeare seems to be using Cicero merely as an informed onstage spectator (he does not reappear in the play). His question alerts the theatre audience to Caesar's meeting with the Roman senators on the next day, the very day the Soothsayer had warned Caesar to beware of – the Ides of March.

With Cicero's departure from the stage, Cassius enters. Unlike Casca, who finds the storm frightening, and Cicero, who seems to consider it merely uncomfortable, Cassius seeks the very centre of it. He refuses to show any fear of it, presenting himself 'Even in the aim and very flash' of its lightning. For Cassius, the storm holds important meanings. If Casca 'would consider the true cause' of all these strange and disturbing omens, he would recognise them as the warning of social upheaval in Rome itself. For Cassius, the night also foreshadows the tyranny which threatens Rome if Caesar is crowned:

> Now could I, Casca, name to thee a man
> Most like this dreadful night,
> That thunders, lightens, opens graves, and roars
> As doth the lion in the Capitol *(lines 72–5)*

Cleverly, Cassius prompts Casca to name the man he is referring to. Casca's ''Tis Caesar that you mean, is it not, Cassius?' opens the way for Cassius to recall the Rome of the former generation, and to point out that 'Romans now' still have the qualities and strength of their ancestors. What they now lack is the courage and determination of their forefathers, who drove out the earlier tyrants and established Rome as a Republic:

> And we are governed with our mothers' spirits;
> Our yoke and sufferance show us womanish. *(lines 83–4)*

For Cassius, there is an essential dignity in calling oneself a Roman. It is a dignity which cannot be compromised by submitting to the decrees of a dictator. Rather than see his honour and dignity besmirched, the noble Roman will readily take his own life.

When Casca tells Cassius of the possibility that Caesar will be crowned and recognised as a king 'In every place save here in Italy', Cassius answers:

> I know where I will wear this dagger then:
> Cassius from bondage will deliver Cassius.　　(lines 89–90)

In the ten lines that follow, Cassius seems to celebrate suicide as a last resort in which the weak can triumph over the strong. No imprisonment of the body, he says, 'Can be retentive to the strength of spirit'. In the final lines of this speech Cassius throws out a declaration and a challenge:

> If I know this, know all the world besides,
> That part of tyranny that I do bear
> I can shake off at pleasure.　　(lines 98–100)

This commitment to death rather than enduring tyranny is endorsed by Casca, who sees suicide as a universal option available to 'every bondman'. Having persuaded Casca thus far, Cassius turns again to Caesar's tyranny over Rome. He claims that the unchecked growth of Caesar's power is due not to any quality in him, but to the submissiveness of Rome's citizens. Why does he suddenly check the flow of his criticism of Rome and Caesar with 'But, O grief, / Where hast thou led me?' Once again, as in Scenes 1 and 2, Shakespeare hints that in Caesar's Rome, men must be very wary of speaking openly to one another. Does Cassius genuinely doubt Casca's trustworthiness? Might there be a deliberate and calculated taunt in his conjecture, 'I perhaps speak this / Before a willing bondman'?

Casca certainly seems quick to declare that he is not 'a willing bondman' who would betray Cassius' confidence, and is eager to join any plot against Caesar:

> You speak to Casca, and to such a man
> That is no fleering tell-tale. Hold, my hand.
> Be factious for redress of all these griefs,
> And I will set this foot of mine as far
> As who goes farthest.　　(lines 116–20)

Now that Casca's commitment has been secured, Cassius tells him that he has already recruited 'Some certain of the noblest-minded Romans' to join the conspiracy and that they wait for him to meet them 'In Pompey's Porch'. For him now, the storm-shaken night resembles 'the work we have in hand, / Most bloody, fiery, and most terrible'.

The rapidity with which the conspiracy has gathered strength is shown dramatically by the arrival of Cinna. He comes 'in haste' to seek Cassius. The necessary secrecy of the plot is emphasised by the seeming breathlessness with which the three men greet and identify each other. The last 25 lines of the scene emphasise the three men's desire to secure the committed participation of Brutus in the conspiracy to overthrow Caesar. Cassius, again the leading organiser, delegates to Cinna the task of leaving forged letters where Brutus will find them. But Shakespeare makes it clear that Brutus will head a sizeable group of conspirators. Amid the planned bustle which aims to consolidate the conspirators, he carefully inserts the names of Decius Brutus, Trebonius and Metellus Cimber, each of whom will later be instrumental in the assassination of Caesar. Yet he also establishes Cassius as the joint leader of the conspiracy, confident that Brutus will soon join: 'the man entire / Upon the next encounter yields him ours'.

Casca's final lines in the scene make clear to the theatre audience why the support of Brutus is indispensable. Brutus' open involvement will give dignity and idealism to a bloody assassination, transforming it to an act committed in the interests of a government worthy of Rome:

> O, he sits high in all the people's hearts,
> And that which would appear offence in us
> His countenance, like richest alchemy,
> Will change to virtue and to worthiness.   *(lines 157–60)*

Act 1: Critical review

Act I reveals the precarious loyalties beneath the apparent stability of Rome's politics. The plebeians are established from the start as being a significant element in the action of the play. Important questions emerge about just how the common people relate to those who govern them. How much trust can be placed in the expressed will of 'the people'? How lasting or how momentary is popular support likely to be? How much moral seriousness do the common people invest in their political function?

Caesar is introduced through the comments of others, especially Cassius and Casca, but Shakespeare affords two brief glimpses of the man himself. The man we see is no longer youthful, is troubled by epilepsy and by deafness, and is, for all his masculinity of stature, deprived of fatherhood. The public figure he has to cultivate as Roman emperor is at odds with his awareness of his humanity. He seems a shrewd judge of his enemies, and identifies with precision the qualities and energy of the man who will engineer his destruction. Yet he emerges also as a man capable of cultivating warm friendships. In all, there is nothing in this act to persuade an audience to accept Cassius' assessment of him.

Friendship assumes a growing importance as the action unfolds. That between Brutus and Caesar is only glanced at. But Caesar's liking for – and trust in – Antony is strongly established in the brief glimpses of them together. Yet in the day-to-day politics of Rome there are perils in friendship too. The genuineness of the friendship between Cassius and Brutus seems sound, but by the end of Act I Cassius seems to have used the obligations of friendship to secure Brutus' support for the conspiracy.

The physical infirmities of Caesar, the introspection of Brutus and the neurotic energy of Cassius reflect the unsettled political conditions of Rome. Shakespeare relates the uneasy states of mind and body with the storm, so widening the play's universe.

The act is dominated by Cassius. His ability to bring together men of diverse dispositions and predilections arises from his astute perception of their individual fears and needs, his obsessive vitality and his capacity to use occasion.

Act 2 Scene 1

> What, Lucius, ho!
> I cannot by the progress of the stars
> Give guess how near to day.   *(lines 1–3)*

The opening lines that Brutus speaks would impress upon a theatre
audience in Shakespeare's time that this scene is set at night, and that
light and darkness are important dramatic elements in the play.
Lucius (whose name itself is close to the Latin word for 'light') is sent
to bring light to Brutus' study.

It is made clear to the theatre audience from Brutus' yearning
comment, 'I would it were my fault to sleep so soundly' that Brutus
has spent a sleepless night. Alone on the stage, he wrestles with the
difficult decision he has to make. The short opening sentence of his
soliloquy reveals his conclusion that only by killing Caesar can his
growing power be checked: 'It must be by his death.'

He then sets about persuading himself that this planned
assassination is justified not out of personal resentment, but for the
greater good of Rome. Indeed, the whole of Brutus' soliloquy turns on
weighing his personal knowledge of Caesar's character against the
way Caesar may change if he is crowned:

> I know no personal cause to spurn at him
> But for the general. He would be crowned:
> How that might change his nature, there's the question.
>   *(lines 11–13)*

There is deep dramatic irony in Brutus' next two lines. In Brutus'
mind 'the adder' represents the dangerous tyrant Caesar might
become. He is unaware that the lines he speaks might aptly refer to
what he (Brutus) is in the process of becoming:

> It is the bright day that brings forth the adder
> And that craves wary walking.   *(lines 14–15)*

As Brutus sees it, 'the bright day' refers to Caesar's possible
coronation. For the conspirators, it could also be the day of Caesar's
assassination.

Again Brutus admits that his personal knowledge of Caesar gives him no cause to act against him. He has no evidence of Caesar's failure to judge with rationality and fairness. His case against Caesar rests on suspicion of what Caesar 'may' become. In the last seven lines of the soliloquy, Brutus seems to surrender the honest, fair side of his nature. He admits that Caesar has not yet misused his power, but Brutus persuades himself that

> since the quarrel
> Will bear no colour for the thing he is,
> Fashion it thus: that what he is, augmented,
> Would run to these and these extremities.   *(lines 28–31)*

Rather than rely on his regard for Caesar as a friend and fellow Roman, Brutus acts very much like a tyrant. He chooses to judge Caesar as a dangerous threat, and he arrives at the conclusion with which his soliloquy began:

> And therefore think him as a serpent's egg
> (Which, hatched, would as his kind grow mischievous)
> And kill him in the shell.   *(lines 32–4)*

Lucius has found one of the letters that Cassius has written to encourage Brutus to join the conspiracy. Brutus sends him to confirm that the coming day is the Ides of March. There are reminders in the dialogue of the darkness, but also of the unusually bright meteors in the sky, by whose light Brutus reads the letter. The dramatic importance of Brutus' being unable to sleep is sharpened by the resonance of the words he reads:

> 'Brutus, thou sleep'st. Awake, and see thyself!'   *(line 46)*

The letter does not specify what should be done, but prompts Brutus to 'piece it out'. He does so, and makes his decision to act against Caesar with a new-found certainty:

> Am I entreated
> To speak and strike? O Rome, I make thee promise,
> If the redress will follow, thou receivest
> Thy full petition at the hand of Brutus.   *(lines 55–8)*

Shakespeare's technique in this scene is to keep two levels of dramatic activity running at the same time. He contrasts the youthful innocence of Lucius with the dark, disturbed struggle in Brutus' mind, and he sets the constant entrances and exits of Lucius against the sustained presence and contemplation of Brutus on the stage. As instructed, Lucius returns to confirm that the coming day is indeed the Ides of March.

Lucius has prepared the light in Brutus' study, but Brutus is held in the darkness by the arrival of the conspirators. The moments between the knock on the door and the entrance of the conspirators are agonising for Brutus. He seems to hold Cassius responsible for his sleepless nights, as he recognises the battle that has raged within him since first he considered the need to assassinate Caesar. He sees the conflict in his own mind in political terms, the soul and body locked in debate:

> The genius and the mortal instruments
> Are then in council, and the state of a man,
> Like to a little kingdom, suffers then
> The nature of an insurrection.   *(lines 66–9)*

Lucius enters once more to announce the arrival of the conspirators, all of whom (except Cassius) have their faces muffled. In the brief time between Lucius' exit to admit the conspirators and their entrance, Brutus acknowledges the shame of being part of a conspiracy:

> O conspiracy,
> Sham'st thou to show thy dang'rous brow by night,
> When evils are most free? O then by day
> Where wilt thou find a cavern dark enough
> To mask thy monstrous visage?   *(lines 77–81)*

From now on, he realises, he will no longer be able to reveal his true thoughts and feelings. He must dissemble, disguising his new role as a murderer 'in smiles and affability'.

Cassius introduces Brutus to the conspirators, then draws him aside to speak in confidence. As a dramatic device, this enables Shakespeare to add cosmic symbolism by busying Decius, Casca and

Cinna in anticipating where the first light of morning will show itself. The day of Caesar's murder is dawning, and Casca, pointing with his sword at where the sun will rise, gives the day its special significance. Some productions give an alternative resonance to the lines, having Casca point his sword directly towards Brutus.

When Cassius and Brutus join the gathering again, Brutus' leadership is evident. He shakes the hands of the other conspirators 'one by one', and promptly overrules Cassius' suggestion that they swear an oath of commitment. He says that even the thought that an oath is necessary would 'stain / The even virtue of our enterprise'. For Brutus, a Roman's word is his bond:

> every drop of blood
> That every Roman bears, and nobly bears,
> Is guilty of a several bastardy
> If he do break the smallest particle
> Of any promise that hath passed from him.   *(lines 136–40)*

The authority that Brutus now holds among the conspirators is further shown as he overturns Cassius' next suggestion – that Cicero be brought into the conspiracy: 'he will never follow anything / That other men begin.'

For the conspirators, the most important question raised at this meeting concerns the fate of Caesar's friend, Mark Antony. Again, it is Cassius who judges Antony to be a political opportunist ('A shrewd contriver') with the potential to become a serious threat. 'Let Antony and Caesar fall together', he urges. Brutus argues against Cassius' proposal for two reasons. First, he wants the murder of Caesar to appear a sad necessity rather than a vicious killing. 'Let's be sacrificers, but not butchers,' he says to Cassius. He shows his deeply felt reluctance to kill as he claims it is the spirit of Caesar which they oppose:

> O, that we then could come by Caesar's spirit
> And not dismember Caesar! But, alas,
> Caesar must bleed for it.   *(lines 169–71)*

Second, he judges Antony to be an insignificant force on his own, counting him as one whose every act is governed by Caesar:

And for Mark Antony, think not of him,
For he can do no more than Caesar's arm
When Caesar's head is off.   *(lines 181–3)*

Ironically, Brutus' dismissal of Cassius' fear of Antony echoes
Antony's own earlier poor judgement of Cassius.

The clock strikes three. The early hour and Cassius' momentary
feeling that Caesar might allow superstition to persuade him to stay at
home remind the theatre audience that the conspiracy's success still
depends, to some extent, upon chance. Decius assures them that he
knows how to persuade Caesar to come to the Capitol. Cassius, Brutus
and Cinna agree to arrive at Caesar's house at eight o'clock in the
morning, to fetch him. When the conspirators are on the point of
leaving, Metellus seems suddenly to remember that Caius Ligarius
bears a grudge against Caesar for little more than a rebuke, and
proposes that he be included in the conspiracy. It is a suggestion that
Brutus accepts, urging Metellus to 'Send him but hither and I'll
fashion him.' In his farewell to the conspirators, Brutus (who earlier
had unhappily accepted the need to disguise his own thoughts in
joviality) urges them similarly to hide their intentions from others:

Good gentlemen, look fresh and merrily:
Let not our looks put on our purposes,
But bear it as our Roman actors do,
With untired spirits and formal constancy.   *(lines 224–8)*

The last two lines are Shakespeare's way of reminding his audience of
the theatricality of the re-enactment they are witnessing.

Left alone, Brutus notices the sleeping Lucius, who, unlike Brutus,
is still able to 'Enjoy the honey-heavy dew of slumber.' But Brutus'
strong participation in the conspiracy seems now to have distanced
him irrevocably from the boy-servant, whose youth, freedom from the
deviousness of politics and innocence he so envies.

Yet Shakespeare presents Brutus with one further test of his
commitment to the aims of the conspiracy: his wife Portia. Her
entrance after the departure of the conspirators surprises Brutus, who
is concerned about her health. She counters this by expressing at
length her anxiety about Brutus, his own unusual disregard for her
and his angry impatience, which, she hoped, 'was but an effect of

humour / Which sometime hath his hour with every man'. But she has concluded that the cause of his behaviour must lie deeper:

> It will not let you eat nor talk nor sleep;
> And could it work so much upon your shape
> As it hath much prevailed on your condition,
> I should not know you, Brutus. *(lines 252–5)*

Portia is not for a moment fooled by Brutus' 'I am not well in health, and that is all.' She senses that Brutus does not suffer in his body, but that his condition is psychological, and feels that she has a right to his confidence:

> You have some sick offence within your mind,
> Which by the right and virtue of my place
> I ought to know of. *(lines 268–70)*

Portia also demands to know who Brutus' visitors were: 'Some six or seven who did hide their faces / Even from darkness.' She feels so excluded from what now seems to govern Brutus' life that she questions the nature of their relationship and the meaning of their marriage:

> Dwell I but in the suburbs
> Of your good pleasure? If it be no more
> Portia is Brutus' harlot, not his wife. *(lines 285–7)*

As a proof of her devotion to Brutus, Portia reveals a terrible self-inflicted wound (see page 98), prompting Brutus to ask the gods to make him 'worthy of this noble wife'. Whether Brutus is genuinely stricken with remorse or not is open to question. Some stage productions have suggested guilt and sincerity; others not. The moment is interrupted by the arrival of Caius Ligarius, but before sending Portia away, Brutus promises to share with her 'All the charactery of my sad brows'.

Sickness in different forms has become an important dramatic element in the play. Wrestling with his conscience has taken its toll on Brutus' health, just as Brutus' self-absorption has affected the mind and body of Portia. Now Lucius announces Ligarius as 'a sick man that

would speak with you'. In the closing 24 lines of the scene, Ligarius'
bodily sickness is healed by his new state of mind as he eagerly puts
himself under Brutus' leadership. Pulling off his bandage, he
declares, 'I here discard my sickness!' While neither of the men
speaks directly of the task in hand, they seem to have an unspoken
understanding. Brutus, thinking pre-eminently of the good of Rome,
describes the planned assassination as 'A piece of work that will make
sick men whole', but Ligarius' answer identifies more ominously what
must be done:

> But are not some whole that we must make sick? *(line 328)*

The dramatic significance of Ligarius has two aspects. The first is
his recovery and his new vitality; the second is his endorsing the
leadership and the responsibility of Brutus for the coming murder.
For Ligarius, 'it sufficeth / That Brutus leads me on'. Some critics also
find significance in the roll of thunder after his last line, arguing that
it sets the seal on Brutus' leadership of the conspiracy, suggests that
Caesar's death is now inevitable and foreshadows the consequences
that will later break apart the foundations of order in Rome.

Act 2 Scene 2

'Nor heaven nor earth have been at peace tonight.' The opening line,
together with a peal of thunder, carries the effects of the stormy night
into the household of Caesar. It is now dawn. Calpurnia has dreamed
of Caesar's murder, and her crying out about it in her sleep has made
him uneasy. He sends a servant to the priests, who will, after a ritual
of sacrifice, give some indication of Caesar's fortune.

Caesar is still torn by the conflict between an instinctive awareness
of the danger he is in and the fearless image he has to project. To
Calpurnia's insistence that he stay at home, Caesar replies with scorn
that he has never been afraid to confront danger:

> The things that threatened me
> Ne'er looked but on my back; when they shall see
> The face of Caesar they are vanishèd. *(lines 10–12)*

Calpurnia is very open in admitting her fear. She not only fears the
predictions of the priests, but also, and with greater urgency, the

report of 'most horrid sights seen by the watch'. The sequence of images which Calpurnia recounts bears some resemblance to what Casca described in Act 1 Scene 3, but is more focused on cataclysmic disaster. In both the natural and the supernatural worlds there have been abnormal events. Lion cubs have been born in the streets and the dead have risen from their graves, while armies fought upon the clouds and 'drizzled blood upon the Capitol'. The sounds, too, suggest a general chaos:

> Horses did neigh and dying men did groan,
> And ghosts did shriek and squeal about the streets. *(lines 23–4)*

Calpurnia's stress on the extraordinary nature of these nightmare images and her admission 'I do fear them' brings nothing but a stubborn dismissal from Caesar. He argues that any prophecies in these unnatural events are not directed exclusively at him, but at the world in general. He is unmoved by Calpurnia's warning that the heavens reserve such displays for rulers and princes, though some actors have brought a moment of thoughtfulness to Caesar's next lines:

> Of all the wonders that I yet have heard
> It seems to me most strange that men should fear,
> Seeing that death, a necessary end,
> Will come when it will come. *(lines 34–7)*

In so doing, they have Caesar reveal a deeper level of reflection than he has thus far shown. More often, the comment is delivered to reinforce Caesar's arrogant contempt for those who admit to a fear of death. Arguably, there is also an unconscious prophetic element in Caesar's observation.

The servant reports that the priests were unable to find a heart within the sacrificed beast, and they warn Caesar not to leave his house that morning. Caesar is quick to interpret the finding in his own way. He claims that it means he would be lacking heart or courage if he feared to leave his house, and he insists that he will go to the Capitol. Calpurnia's response shows her understanding of Caesar. She makes a perceptive judgement of him and offers a way for Caesar to reconsider his decision without losing face:

> Alas, my lord,
> Your wisdom is consumed in confidence.
> Do not go forth today. Call it my fear
> That keeps you in the house, and not your own. *(lines 48–51)*

She suggests that Mark Antony will make a convincing excuse, saying that Caesar is unwell. Her tactic succeeds. Caesar accepts this, conceding that Calpurnia's anxiety has changed his mind. A theatre director has to decide how to show this agreement. Does Caesar agree because he fears for his own safety? Does he genuinely wish to ease Calpurnia's anguish? Or is he merely humouring her, quickly but decisively?

Caesar immediately makes the newly arrived Decius the messenger and orders him to tell the senators that Caesar will not be there. No excuse is necessary:

> Cannot is false, and that I dare not, falser:
> I will not come today. Tell them so, Decius. *(lines 63–4)*

Decius has assured the conspirators that he will bring Caesar to the Capitol (Act 2 Scene 1, line 211). Caesar's refusal to lie is very typical of the self-confidence – perhaps arrogance – that has governed his responses thus far. Decius is quick to seize the opportunity to argue that, without an explanation, he will be laughed at, whereupon Caesar, in another show of arrogance, insists:

> The cause is in my will. I will not come:
> That is enough to satisfy the Senate. *(lines 71–2)*

For Decius alone, he offers the explanation that his decision has been prompted by Calpurnia and her dream. Decius counters with a new and deliberately flattering interpretation of the dream. The blood pouring from his statue does not signify disaster. Rather, it means that Caesar's blood gives life and strength to the citizens of Rome.

Decius then adds further possible consequences if Caesar stays at home. First, he says that the Senate has planned to offer Caesar a crown, and that his failure to attend might change their minds. Second, he stresses the mockery that will be prompted by delaying the Senate meeting until '"Caesar's wife shall meet with better dreams."'

Third, he suggests that if Caesar appears to 'hide himself' it will be concluded that 'Caesar is afraid'. These three arguments show that Decius does indeed know how to persuade Caesar by working upon his ambition for power and upon his sensitivity about being thought ridiculous or fearful.

Caesar immediately turns on Calpurnia, blaming her, perhaps in jest, for his change of mind, and preparing to set off for the Capitol. He is forestalled by the arrival of the other conspirators, in whose company he becomes a genial host. He greets them each by name, taking a moment to acknowledge, jokingly, that Caius Ligarius' poor health had left more serious marks on him than any quarrel between them. He directs a jovial greeting to Mark Antony, and then singles out Trebonius, for whom he has 'an hour's talk in store', and whom he urges to 'Be near me that I may remember you.'

In selecting Caius Ligarius, Mark Antony and Trebonius for special mention at this point, Shakespeare makes Caesar especially vulnerable. Ligarius' bitterness is more enduring than Caesar knows. Antony will be deliberately led away from the Capitol, and Trebonius grimly enjoys the unconscious irony in Caesar's words.

Calpurnia's warning about wisdom being displaced by confidence gathers a special resonance as Caesar, with sweeping self-assurance, is surrounded by those who pretend affection and loyalty, but who will kill him, and to them he proposes a ceremonious gesture of friendship:

> Good friends, go in and taste some wine with me,
> And we, like friends, will straightway go together.
>
> *(lines 126–7)*

It is the classic prelude to betrayal, the unknowing victim drinking wine with his killers. Brutus is struck by Caesar's use of the word 'like'. He comments in an aside on the rift between the conspirators' false show of friendship and the genuineness of their murderous intent:

> That every like is not the same, O Caesar,
> The heart of Brutus earns to think upon. *(lines 128–9)*

This is his private acknowledgement of his own personal grief and guilt for the act of betrayal (in Shakespeare's time, 'earns' had the meaning of 'yearns' or 'grieves').

Act 2 Scene 3

In this very brief scene, Artemidorus, a character who has not appeared in the play till now, reads out the written warning he plans to give to Caesar. It makes clear that the odds against Caesar are high. Plutarch (see page 65) records that Artemidorus was not by birth a Roman, but was

> born in the isle of Gnidos, a doctor of rhetoric in the Greek
> tongue, who by means of his profession was very familiar with
> certain of Brutus' confederates and therefore knew the most
> part of all their practices against Caesar, came and brought
> him a little bill written with his own hand, of all that he meant
> to tell him.

Shakespeare makes Artemidorus more memorable, more interesting and dramatically more important by giving him a whole scene to himself. The scene is neatly divided into prose and verse. It was a stage convention for letters to be written in prose, and accordingly the first half of the scene is taken up with Artemidorus reading the written warning he intends to give to Caesar. He clearly knows the plans for Caesar's assassination in some detail, for he names the seven important conspirators, and is aware of what has brought Caius Ligarius into their number. He also knows that for all their different personalities, 'There is but one mind in all these men, and it is bent against Caesar.'

In the last six lines Artemidorus considers how he hopes to put this letter into Caesar's hand. He meditates on the sad fact that 'virtue cannot live / Out of the teeth of emulation': high-minded men like Caesar are inevitably threatened by those who envy their position and seek to destroy them. Finally, Artemidorus acknowledges that his letter can save Caesar, but if Caesar does not read it, then destiny has sided with the conspirators:

> If thou read this, O Caesar, thou mayst live;
> If not, the fates with traitors do contrive.   *(lines 12–13)*

With those lines, Artemidorus leaves the stage. He will appear only once more, jostled by the crowd, to speak three lines. His note will be ignored and he will be brushed aside by Caesar and by those who surround him. The hopelessness of Artemidorus' cause is dramatised by Shakespeare in placing him in this scene to stand alone against the sweep of power that the conspiracy has gathered in the preceding two scenes. But he is dramatically important because his view of Caesar is so clearly different from that of the conspirators. Shakespeare is offering his audience another assessment of Caesar. For Artemidorus, Caesar is a man of 'virtue'– a word that in Shakespeare's time meant both 'manliness' and 'goodness'.

Act 2 Scene 4

As in the preceding scene, the setting for the action is a Roman street. This scene is dominated by Portia, who, in a state of agitation and confusion, seems torn between sending Lucius on a bewildering, unspecific errand to the Capitol and controlling her impulse to speak of what is in her mind. She acknowledges 'How hard it is for women to keep counsel!' in her aside, then turns to find Lucius not yet gone. Her sentences are short and breathless, and she gives Lucius the task of observing the condition of Brutus who 'went sickly forth'. She seems aware that what is to be done at the Capitol is the key to Brutus' state of health. She also charges Lucius to 'take good note / What Caesar doth, what suitors press to him'.

Portia's disturbed state of mind heightens suspense at this point. She is quick to attach significance to what her senses perceive:

> I heard a bustling rumour, like a fray,
> And the wind brings it from the Capitol.   *(lines 18–19)*

Perhaps Portia's intuition makes her keenly aware of an ominous meaning in what she has observed – the mysterious men who came to Brutus during the night, his sleeplessness and loss of appetite, the speed with which Brutus sent her away when Ligarius arrived. Yet her instruction to Lucius to observe particularly Brutus and Caesar and those who crowd upon him might suggest that she knows some details of the conspiracy.

Shakespeare dramatises his portrayal of her inner conflict from what he read in Plutarch:

> Portia being very careful and pensive for that which was to
> come and being too weak to away with so great and inward

grief of mind, she could hardly keep within, but was frighted
with every little noise and cry she heard . . . asking every man
that came from the market-place what Brutus did, and still sent
messenger after messenger to know what news.

In contrast to Portia's agitation and to Lucius' uncertainty, the
Soothsayer brings a resigned serenity with his entrance. No longer is
his voice 'shriller than all the music' as Caesar described it in Act 1
Scene 2. He answers Portia's questions with a quiet, measured
courtesy and seems to indicate that only Caesar can now shape his
immediate destiny. The Soothsayer seems to recognise that Caesar's
arrogance will finally thrust him towards his own destruction. He will
offer words of advice, which he implies will benefit Caesar if Caesar
will only listen:

> if it will please Caesar
> To be so good to Caesar as to hear me   *(lines 28–9)*

He also implies that what has made Caesar so unsuspecting a victim
is his inability to distinguish enemies from those he can trust. 'I shall
beseech him to befriend himself' suggests that Caesar is his own
worst enemy.

Another change in the Soothsayer is his new role, more an
observer than a prophet. He prepares to stand and watch Caesar 'pass
on to the Capitol'. When Portia asks him if he knows of any intention
to harm Caesar, his reply is again worded with ominous undertones:

> None that I know will be, much that I fear may chance.
>
> *(line 32)*

The best he can now do is to find an uncrowded spot where he might
'Speak to great Caesar as he comes along.'

In the last eight lines of the scene Portia's anxiety becomes most
acute. Shakespeare invites the audience to ponder just what Portia
does know. Does she, or does she not know that Brutus is part of a
conspiracy to assassinate Caesar? Just what might she mean by
'enterprise' when she exclaims 'O Brutus, / The heavens speed thee in
thine enterprise!'?

Act 2: Critical review

The first scene of this act is dominated by Brutus. In contrast with the public setting of the earlier action, the domestic life of the Romans is introduced. The privacy of Brutus' home is invaded by the conspiracy in three ways: first by his own dilemma, which emerges in his soliloquy; second by the letters thrown in through his window; and third by the arrival of the conspirators themselves. Brutus' soliloquies show his mental agony. The meeting of the conspirators at Brutus' home involves him irrevocably in the plot to kill Caesar, yet his judgement on important issues – Antony's fate, the exclusion of Cicero and the inclusion of Ligarius – is impulsive and idealistic rather than cautious. Brutus seems to be at the centre of a struggle between the secret group of conspirators, and the two constant figures of his household – Lucius, with his quiet devotion, and Portia, with her insistent appeal for his confidence.

The opposing conditions of sickness and health, touched on in the earlier scenes, are reinforced here, with Brutus and Ligarius representing their manifestation in both body and mind. Brutus might also be seen as the centre of a symbolic tussle between light and darkness.

Like Brutus, Caesar is presented in an uneasy state of mind and in his own home. Caesar also seems to be at the centre of a struggle between Calpurnia's anxieties and his obligations to the Roman senators. Calpurnia's dream is rich in visual images, especially those involving blood, and so is resoundingly prophetic. Her insight into Caesar's mind enables her to prevail briefly, and so to present one chance of saving Caesar. But Caesar's final decision to go to the Senate arises from characteristic elements revealed earlier: his fear of being seen as indecisive, and his dread of ridicule. In a brief moment of magnanimity he invites his prepared assassins to taste wine with him 'like friends'.

Shakespeare sustains suspense as Artemidorus plans to warn Caesar by letter of the danger that threatens him, so presenting a second possibility of frustrating the conspiracy. Portia's agitation suggests that she is aware of Brutus' involvement in the planned murder. The Soothsayer reappears and is deliberately enigmatic.

Act 3 Scene 1

As Caesar moves towards the situation his murderers have planned for him he becomes increasingly self-confident. His challenge to the Soothsayer – 'The Ides of March are come' – is often delivered mockingly on the stage, but the Soothsayer's response that the day is not yet over carries both an acknowledgement of Caesar's joking defiance and an ominous caution. Artemidorus, in his urgent attempt to put his letter of warning into Caesar's hand, calls on him directly to 'Read this schedule', but he is forestalled by Decius' much more servile appeal:

> Trebonius doth desire you to o'er-read
> (At your best leisure) this his humble suit.   *(lines 4–5)*

Again, Artemidorus urges Caesar to read his letter, because its content 'touches Caesar nearer'. In response, Caesar delivers the line that seals his fate:

> What touches us ourself shall be last served.   *(line 8)*

Does this reveal a genuine unselfishness in Caesar, or is it a moment of supreme arrogance? This is a moment where Shakespeare can be seen to have changed what he read for dramatic purposes. Plutarch records that Caesar took Artemidorus' letter and actually tried to read it, but the welcoming crowds pressing around him prevented him from doing so. Shakespeare increases dramatic tension as Caesar's grandiloquent reply to Artemidorus puts him beyond the reach of rescue. Publius and Cassius brush Artemidorus aside as Caesar enters the Capitol.

Shakespeare heightens the tension by having Popillius wish Cassius success with today's 'enterprise'. Cassius instantly fears that the conspiracy is no longer a guarded secret. He anxiously urges Casca not to delay the first strike against Caesar, and threatens suicide if the plot is discovered. The difference in character between Brutus and Cassius is further revealed as Brutus calms Cassius' extreme anxiety, pointing out that Caesar shows no alarm as Popillius speaks to him.

The well-planned sequence of moves is carried out. Trebonius removes Mark Antony at the right moment, Decius arranges for Metellus Cimber to approach Caesar with his request, and Cinna urges Casca to strike the first blow. As soon as Caesar sets in motion the presentation of requests, Metellus Cimber appeals to 'Most high, most mighty, and most puissant Caesar'. His obsequious address is calculated to rouse Caesar's scorn, and it succeeds as Caesar dismissively rejects the appeal:

> Be not fond
> To think that Caesar bears such rebel blood
> That will be thawed from the true quality
> With that which melteth fools – I mean sweet words,
> Low-crookèd curtsies, and base spaniel fawning.   *(lines 39–43)*

Metellus Cimber appeals for others to reinforce his plea that Caesar reprieve his brother's banishment. Brutus and Cassius support Metellus Cimber, pleading with deliberate and exaggerated servility. Their tactic is to incite Caesar's contempt for them and stir his pride. They succeed. Caesar is provoked into an arrogant boast. Other men are like shifting stars in the heavens; he is the only fixed star, exceptional in his firmness of purpose:

> But I am constant as the northern star,
> Of whose true-fixed and resting quality
> There is no fellow in the firmament.   *(lines 60–2)*

By making so exaggerated a plea for a reprieve for Publius Cimber, the assassins have manoeuvred Caesar into the stance of a tyrant. Making his inflexibility a virtue, Caesar has condemned himself. He insists that he was decisive in banishing Publius Cimber, 'And constant do remain to keep him so.'

The moment of the assassination is an intensely dramatic episode, and all productions work out its staging to intensify theatrical effect. For example, one production took note of Caesar's deafness in his left ear and had him turn to catch the last appeals of Cinna and Decius, so exposing his back to Casca, who first raises his knife with 'Speak hands for me!' Staggering under the knife-thrusts of those around him, Caesar is finally stabbed by Brutus, and utters his final comment: 'Et tu, Brute? – Then fall, Caesar!' His question (Even you, Brutus?) is one of disbelief. His death seems caused as much by Brutus' betrayal as by the stab-wounds inflicted on him. Plutarch observes that Caesar's body finally fell at the base of Pompey's statue, so that the image seemed to take 'just revenge on Pompey's enemy'. Following Plutarch's description, the Mankiewicz film adaptation of the play shows the assassination at the foot of Pompey's statue. For an Elizabethan audience, the murder of a ruler before their eyes would be profoundly shocking. Moreover, like Caesar, Queen Elizabeth I was childless, so there was no heir by birth. The fear of civil strife over the succession was very real.

The first action of the conspirators is to make known the death of Caesar. But they are eager to portray the assassination as an emancipation of Rome from the rule of the tyrant. Both Cinna and Cassius proclaim the words, 'Liberty!' and 'Freedom!' In dramatic contrast to the secrecy of the planning of the conspiracy, both urge those near them to 'cry' these words in public places. Brutus' reaction is again typically more composed. He is concerned that those who have witnessed the killing and who might panic should pause and reflect on the meaning of Caesar's death:

> People and senators, be not affrighted,
> Fly not, stand still! Ambition's debt is paid.   *(lines 82–3)*

Plutarch mentions some senators who 'were so amazed with the horrible sight they saw, they had no power to fly'. Shakespeare concentrates the paralysed reaction of those people in the old senator, Publius. Both Brutus and Cassius advise him to leave, and explain to the people that the conspirators intend no further harm to anyone.

With only the conspirators left on stage, Shakespeare is careful to keep alive an awareness of Mark Antony, earlier led away from the scene of the murder by Trebonius. His later entrance is prepared for by Cassius' question, 'Where is Antony?', but the assassins' most important task is to establish their credibility with the Roman public before there is time for any concerted reaction. As a prelude, Brutus and Casca, recognising that their own lives are in peril, develop an argument which reduces life, as Casca maintains, merely to a fear-ridden wait for death:

> Why, he that cuts off twenty years of life
> Cuts off so many years of fearing death.   *(lines 101–2)*

Brutus takes the argument further, declaring that they are 'Caesar's friends, that have abridged / His time of fearing death'. Their words recall Caesar's own words about death and the fear of death. Theatre audiences might also recall Calpurnia's dream as Brutus and Cassius urge the conspirators to soak their hands and arms in Caesar's blood, to parade themselves 'waving our red weapons o'er our heads' and to cry out, 'Peace, freedom, and liberty!' In justifying the murder, they hope to transform Caesar's blood from its association with guilt to a symbol of liberation. Yet there is a powerful irony in the word 'stoop' – used by both Brutus and Cassius – with its suggestion that they are in fact lowering themselves. The irony gains an added depth as Shakespeare typically has Cassius imagine 'our lofty scene' of Caesar's death being re-enacted on stages in the future:

> So oft as that shall be,
> So often shall the knot of us be called
> The men that gave their country liberty. *(lines 116–18)*

Shakespeare too, no doubt enjoyed the thought of his play being performed by future generations of actors.

At the height of their elation, the assassins are approached by a servant bringing from Antony a surprisingly compliant message. Recognising worthy qualities in both Caesar and Brutus, Antony asks that he may safely approach Brutus to learn 'How Caesar hath deserved to lie in death'. In return, he undertakes to 'follow / The fortunes and affairs of noble Brutus'. Interestingly, he makes no acknowledgement of Cassius.

Brutus' response is generous, believing that Antony's friendship is assured. Cassius remains unconvinced of Antony's trustworthiness, but has no time to argue as Antony enters, first paying his respects to the dead Caesar and then inviting Caesar's killers to kill him 'Now, whilst your purpled hands do reek and smoke'. Plutarch records Antony's first meeting with the assassins as taking place a day after Caesar's murder. Shakespeare quickens the pace, tightening dramatic tension, and also presents Antony as a much more formidable character by bringing him to face the conspirators while Caesar's blood is still moist on their hands. His apparent begging for death might be a genuine request, but perhaps it is a challenge, which, Antony shrewdly calculates, will not be taken up. As he declares that he would not wish to die anywhere other than beside Caesar, there is something of a mocking taunt in his description of the conspirators as 'The choice and master spirits of this age'.

The responses of Brutus and Cassius again reveal the differences in their characters. Brutus is at pains to explain that 'Though now we must appear bloody and cruel', the conspirators are, at heart, 'pitiful' (merciful). The killing of Caesar was driven by 'pity to the general wrong of Rome'. He assures Antony that against him, their swords are blunted, having 'leaden points'; that they welcome him 'With all kind love, good thoughts, and reverence'. Cassius is far less effusive. He merely promises Antony that he will have as much influence as anyone in selecting the new leaders of Rome. Perhaps he recognises the political importance of involving Antony promptly in the new dispensation.

Antony accepts Brutus' promise that he will explain 'Why I, that did love Caesar when I struck him, / Have thus proceeded', though his reference to the conspirators' 'wisdom' carries an ambiguous edge. To suggest that they are wise does not involve a judgement of their action, and though some of the conspirators may suspect Antony's careful wording, most may be prepared to accept it. Naming the assassins individually, he shakes the bloody hand of each. He calls Casca (the first to stab Caesar) 'valiant'. Trebonius (who led him away before the killing) he leaves to the last, calling him 'good' and, echoing Brutus' words, assuring him that he is 'not least in love'.

It begins to become clear that Antony is a master politician, seizing the moment to act and turning language to suit his purpose. He is quick to exploit Brutus' offer of friendship, and to play for time to avoid making any commitment of support for the killers:

> Gentlemen all – alas, what shall I say?
> My credit now stands on such slippery ground
> That one of two bad ways you must conceit me,
> Either a coward or a flatterer.   *(lines 190–3)*

He dramatises his predicament by begging the dead Caesar's forgiveness for 'Shaking the bloody fingers' of the killers, by relating the bleeding wounds on Caesar's body to weeping eyes and by depicting Caesar as a hunted stag surrounded and brought to ground by hounds and hunters. Punning on the words 'hart' (a deer) and 'heart' (the central organ of life), the rhyme gives Antony's words a resonance for the theatre audience.

Cassius is quick to see the potential danger of Antony's apparent vacillation between lamentation and good will:

> I blame you not for praising Caesar so,
> But what compact mean you to have with us?
> Will you be pricked in number of our friends,
> Or shall we on and not depend on you? *(lines 214–17)*

Still playing for time, and perhaps sensing in the different temperaments of Cassius and Brutus the fragility of their alliance, Antony capitalises on his wish to be friends with the conspirators and also to grieve over the death of Caesar. He continues to wait for an explanation as to 'Why and wherein Caesar was dangerous'. But now he adds a further implicit condition:

> that I may
> Produce his body to the market-place,
> And in the pulpit, as becomes a friend,
> Speak in the order of his funeral. *(lines 227–30)*

Brutus immediately agrees. Cassius, with equal promptness, takes Brutus aside to make clear his disagreement. Brutus counters with an assurance that he will speak first to explain why it was necessary to kill Caesar, and to insist that what Antony will say has been approved by them. Cassius remains unconvinced. Antony accepts Brutus' conditions. Brutus' political naivety seems to reach its peak in his belief that if he speaks first, he will eclipse Antony. He seems to believe that the justness of his cause will persuade all people to be reasonable and to view the situation as he does.

Antony's true feelings emerge in the soliloquy over Caesar's dead body. Cassius' judgement proves right, for, no longer surrounded by Caesar's murderers, Antony makes it clear that his conciliatory behaviour was a pretence. After asking the dead Caesar's pardon again for seeking a compromise with the killers – whom he now calls 'butchers', an echo of Brutus' response to Cassius – Antony imagines Caesar's wounds

> Which like dumb mouths do ope their ruby lips
> To beg the voice and utterance of my tongue – *(lines 260–1)*

and foresees the civil disorder and chaos that will befall Rome and all Italy. People will become so accustomed to acts of brutality that mothers 'shall but smile' to see their infants dismembered and all compassion will be smothered. Caesar's spirit, accompanied by Ate, the goddess of revenge, will unleash the forces of destruction on a scale that will leave men decomposing without being able to die:

> That this foul deed shall smell above the earth
> With carrion men groaning for burial. *(lines 274–5)*

The arrival of Octavius brings a new mood to the scene. Octavius is a young relative of Julius Caesar. His political perceptiveness had already been recognised. With his imminent arrival, Shakespeare prepares the forces that will be ranged against the conspirators. Antony advises the servant to wait until after Antony has given his funeral address and tested the public reaction to the murderers before reporting back to his master.

Act 3 Scene 2

As he had planned, Brutus now addresses the crowd to justify Caesar's assassination. In his speech, in prose, he deploys powerful and highly rhetorical language to persuade his audience. He asks them to listen to him and to accept the sincerity of his motives, to believe him and to judge him critically if they wish to. To any friend of Caesar's who may be listening, he claims that his own love for Caesar was as strong as any friend's. The reason for his part in the killing of Caesar was that his love for Rome was more important than his love for Caesar. He asks the plebeians if they would rather Caesar continued to govern them so that they would all die slaves, or whether it would be better that Caesar were dead so that they could live as 'freemen'.

Brutus then lists the positive qualities in Caesar's nature: his love as a friend, his good fortune and his 'valour'. And to each of these qualities, Brutus identifies grief, joy and honour, as his own genuine responses. But in Caesar's ambition lay the danger, and for that, Brutus 'slew him'.

Brutus repeats the qualities and his reactions to them. Then he makes three challenges to his listeners:

> Who is here so base that would be a bondman? If any, speak, for him have I offended. Who is here so rude that would not be a Roman? If any, speak, for him have I offended. Who is here so vile that will not love his country? If any, speak, for him have I offended.
>
> *(lines 25–9)*

By using the words, 'base', 'rude' and 'vile' Brutus has made it almost impossible for anyone to take up his challenge. Whether the crowd's 'None, Brutus, none' emerges as a unanimous shout or a general murmur will depend on how the crowd is portrayed in any particular stage production. Brutus takes the crowd's comment as evidence of their endorsement, with the conclusion, 'Then none have I offended.' Whether he genuinely draws this conclusion or whether he imposes it as part of his rhetorical technique will depend on how sympathetically the character of Brutus is interpreted. He assures them that they have the right to treat him as he has treated Caesar, and that in the public record of Caesar's death, Caesar's virtues will not be diminished, nor his faults exaggerated.

Brutus then focuses the crowd's attention on the arrival of Mark Antony with Caesar's body. He makes it clear that Antony, who had no part in the killing of Caesar, would nonetheless have a valued status, as would every citizen, in the new commonwealth of Rome. He prepares to leave the pulpit with the promise that the dagger with which he stabbed his closest friend 'for the good of Rome' is ready for use against him 'when it shall please my country to need my death'.

The substance of Brutus' speech is uncomplicated, but his use of rhetoric is skilful. His first appeal is to 'Romans, countrymen, and lovers'. By 'lovers' he means 'dear friends', but he puts forward the assumption that there is a link which unites the three ideas. Love is bound up most closely with Italy and with Rome. This connection emerges most powerfully in the last two of the three challenges in lines 26–9.

There is, too, a forceful structure to his sentences which makes the end of the sentence echo the opening verb:

> hear me for my cause, and be silent that you may hear. Believe
> me for mine honour, and have respect to mine honour that you
> may believe. Censure me in your wisdom, and awake your
> senses that you may the better judge.   *(lines 13–16)*

In this last appeal, he credits the crowd with wisdom. Is this a
calculated rhetorical device, or are the words spoken sincerely? It is
possible to argue that Brutus is deliberately flattering his listeners, but
his political naivety might well have led him genuinely to believe they
are wise and capable of accepting his rational argument.

He goes on to accept that there may be some who were Caesar's
dear friends, but his language reduces their possible number, moving
from 'If there be any . . .' to 'any dear friend' and finally 'to him I say
that Brutus' love to Caesar was no less than his'. So his language
technique isolates any friend of Caesar's as an individual exception
among the assembly he is addressing.

The response of the plebeians as Brutus descends from the pulpit
is clearly one of enthusiastic general approval. They offer to 'bring him
to his house / With shouts and clamours', and Shakespeare ironically
has them calling for him to 'be Caesar', showing that they have
misunderstood Brutus' purpose in killing a would-be single ruler. But
Brutus calms them and asks them to hear Antony speak and pay
respect to Caesar's corpse. He stresses that it is with the conspirators'
permission that Antony will speak, and asks that he be allowed to
leave alone.

The crowd's approval of Brutus becomes even clearer when Antony
mounts the pulpit and mentions Brutus' name:

4 PLEBEIAN   'Twere best he speak no harm of Brutus here!
1 PLEBEIAN This Caesar was a tyrant.
3 PLEBEIAN   Nay, that's certain:
    We are blest that Rome is rid of him.   *(lines 60–2)*

The opening four lines of Antony's funeral oration are among the
best-known lines that Shakespeare wrote. His initial appeal is
substantially the same as Brutus'. He too uses rhetorical techniques,
but his style is more direct. He asks for his listeners' attention, he
announces that his purpose is 'to bury Caesar, not to praise him', and
he makes the point that men are remembered for their offences while

their virtues are often entombed with their bodies. Caesar will be no exception:

> The evil that men do lives after them,
> The good is oft interrèd with their bones:
> So let it be with Caesar.　　　　　　　　　 *(lines 67–9)*

Antony reminds his listeners that he speaks with the permission 'of Brutus and the rest'. But he adds the word that will recur ironically through his speech: 'honourable'. He acknowledges Brutus as 'an honourable man', and the conspirators as 'honourable men'. Antony presses on to deal with the charge that Brutus had specifically levelled: that Caesar was ambitious. He speaks of Caesar's qualities as a friend, his military success, his compassion for the poor, his refusal of the offered crown. Against each of Caesar's virtues he raises Brutus' accusation that Caesar was ambitious, and he deepens the irony with each repeated reference to Brutus' reputation as 'an honourable man'.

Using another familiar persuasive technique, Antony claims that he does not seek to undermine Brutus' words, but to speak from his own knowledge of Caesar. He reminds the crowd that they all had held Caesar in high regard with good reason, yet now they show no sign of grief over his death. Momentarily seeming to despair over the crowd's fickleness and apparent lack of reasonable judgement – but in effect appealing to them as men rather than beasts – Antony appears to give way to his own emotion:

> 　　　　　　　　　　Bear with me,
> My heart is in the coffin there with Caesar,
> And I must pause till it come back to me.　　　 *(lines 97–9)*

Antony's rhetoric, a selective blend of Caesar's virtues, of ironic deference to Brutus' honour, of flattery, and of his own distress produces a change in the collective mind of the crowd. Shakespeare deftly gives a range of immediate responses to separate individuals, but they all indicate that the support of the people is deserting Brutus and gathering behind Antony. His deft handling of persuasive language is having the effect he desires.

Antony's pause to gain control of his emotion is evidently part of his calculation. It may look spontaneous, but it is a purposeful action, revealed as such when he speaks again. In drawing the crowd's attention to Caesar's body in the coffin, he reinforces the effect of language with the display of a visible object. He contrasts the world-wide influence of Caesar's words with the small space occupied by his body, focusing awareness of it with 'now lies he there'. On stage, the 'coffin' is often simply the robe covering Caesar's body. Antony chides the plebeians for being too aloof to pay respect to Caesar, and then hints at the response he intends to arouse in them, checking himself once more with an ironic deference to Brutus and Cassius:

> O masters, if I were disposed to stir
> Your hearts and minds to mutiny and rage,
> I should do Brutus wrong and Cassius wrong,
> Who (you all know) are honourable men.   *(lines 113–16)*

Rather than discredit them, Antony claims that he would prefer to dishonour the dead Caesar, himself and his listeners. He has already shown himself a master at focusing the crowd's attention on selected detail. Now he holds up before the plebeians' eyes a crucial piece of evidence of Caesar's generosity: his will. He says he does not intend to read the will's contents, but that if the common people were to hear the will read, they would regard Caesar's body as sacred, bequeathing to their descendants a precious hair of his 'as a rich legacy'.

Antony's device succeeds. By refusing to read the will, he has made his listeners demand to hear it. Antony tantalises them further, saying that he dare not read it, for if they knew Caesar's love for them, they would lose control of their reactions. Echoing the criticism of the common people in the play's opening scene, ironically levelled at them for celebrating Caesar's return to Rome ('You blocks, you stones'), Antony reverses its disparagement:

> You are not wood, you are not stones, but men,
> And, being men, hearing the will of Caesar,
> It will inflame you, it will make you mad.   *(lines 134–6)*

Amid more insistent demands, Antony continues to work on the crowd's craving for the will to be read to them. He asks them to be patient and blames himself for taking matters too far. He protests that he might have defamed 'the honourable men / Whose daggers have stabbed Caesar'. For the first time, Antony links the conspirators with their action of killing Caesar, and this provokes the crowd into fury, denouncing Brutus, Cassius and the other conspirators as 'traitors', 'villains' and 'murderers'.

To the continuing demands that he read the will, Antony has a new response. With his question, 'You will compel me then to read the will?' he seems to put himself under the power of his listeners. (Attributing power to one's audience is another effective rhetorical device.) Assembling them around Caesar's body, he directs their attention to it and then asks their permission to come down from the pulpit. With his 'And will you give me leave?' Antony transfers authority from Brutus and Cassius to the listening plebeians.

Antony now concentrates the attention of the crowd on Caesar's cloak and recalls the first time Caesar wore it:

> 'Twas on a summer's evening, in his tent,
> That day he overcame the Nervii.   *(lines 163–4)*

Antony's selection of detail is cleverly calculated, for the savage Nervii tribe had sprung an ambush on Caesar's army during his Gallic campaign, and his brilliant victory over them had been extravagantly celebrated in Rome. He deliberately reminds the plebeians of Caesar's most memorable conquest before pointing to the gashes in the cloak where the knives of Cassius, 'the envious Casca' and 'the well-belovèd Brutus' had stabbed Caesar. For Brutus, Antony reserves a special place among the murderers:

> For Brutus, as you know, was Caesar's angel.
> Judge, O you gods, how dearly Caesar loved him!
> This was the most unkindest cut of all.   *(lines 172–4)*

With Caesar's fall 'Even at the base of Pompey's statue', Antony claims all the people of Rome have fallen under the triumph of 'bloody treason'. Shakespeare has kept the memory of Pompey in the background since the opening scene of the play. The effect is perhaps to keep a theatre audience alert to the fickleness of crowd loyalty and to play up the irony of Caesar lying at the feet of his former rival.

The plebeians weep. Using their tears as evidence of proper and genuine feelings, Antony turns attention once more to Caesar's body, 'marred as you see with traitors'. The plebeians' response ranges from pity and remorse to a desire for vengeance and unrestrained destruction. Antony skilfully but insincerely pleads for restraint, claiming that he has no wish to rouse them 'To such a sudden flood of mutiny'. He diverts the crowd's attention back to the conspirators, whose reasons for killing Caesar are, he says, not clear to him. Shakespeare's ironic intent is obvious, as Antony claims not to be a speaker with the gifts of Brutus, but only to speak 'as you know me all – a plain blunt man / That love my friend'. All he can do further is to leave Caesar's wounds, 'poor, poor, dumb mouths', to speak for him. Hinting at the crowd's earlier reception of Brutus' funeral oration, Antony says that if he could speak with Brutus' power they would be genuinely stirred to action:

> there were an Antony
> Would ruffle up your spirits and put a tongue
> In every wound of Caesar, that should move
> The stones of Rome to rise and mutiny.   *(lines 217–20)*

Again, the plebeians seem on the verge of sweeping off to find the conspirators and to burn Brutus' house. Again, Antony holds them back by reminding them of Caesar's will, which they have not heard. He tells them that Caesar has left each Roman citizen a sum of money, and to the public and future generations of Romans he has left his private gardens and orchards. This calculated revelation of Caesar's generosity finally drives the crowd into a destructive frenzy. They leave, intent on revenge, and Antony's calculated intention to incite a rebellion against the conspirators becomes clear:

> Now let it work. Mischief, thou art afoot,
> Take thou what course thou wilt!   *(lines 250–1)*

In the last ten lines of the scene, the servant returns to announce that Caesar's young cousin, Octavius, has arrived in Rome, and that Brutus and Cassius have fled through the city gates.

Act 3 Scene 3
This brief scene appears to have been prompted by two sentences from Plutarch, and by Shakespeare's concern to raise important

questions about the relationship between rousing political rhetoric and mob violence.

Plutarch wrote:

> There was one of Caesar's friends called Cinna that had a marvellous, strange and terrible dream the night before. He dreamed that Caesar bade him to supper, and that he refused and would not go; then that Caesar took him by the hand, and led him against his will.

Shakespeare has reshaped Cinna's dream in line with the Elizabethan belief that a happy dream was an omen of ill luck for the dreamer. After dreaming that he 'did feast with Caesar' Cinna's imagination is filled with foreboding and he wanders out into the street. He is surrounded by angry plebeians, who suspect him and are quick to use the new sense of their power. They interrogate him, twist the meaning of his answers and beat him. When he gives his name he is identified as Cinna the conspirator. His protest that he is Cinna the poet does not help him, for the crowd is in no mood to admit the possibility of error. In a frenzied mob they attack and kill him.

The death of Cinna the poet raises important questions. Both Brutus and Antony have in their funeral speeches complimented the plebeians on having qualities of wisdom and kindness. Yet here they set upon an innocent victim, a poet, for whom language is an instrument of sensitivity for the expression of refined thought and feeling. Has Antony been irresponsible in unleashing unthinking destructive forces in his listeners? Do the common people of Rome display to others the freedom that Brutus and Cassius proclaimed for them? Will the new rulers of Rome have to become more tyrannical than Caesar in governing the common people? Is it the nature of politicians to rally people to their own causes rather than to listen to them? Shakespeare confronts his theatre audience with the consequences of volatile, mindless mob violence that can result from the calculating use of political rhetoric.

The scene contains a further irony. The rioting plebeians have been stirred to destructive action by the poetic oratory of Antony. Yet when Cinna desperately identifies himself as 'Cinna the poet', they set upon him with 'Tear him for his bad verses, tear him for his bad verses.'

Act 3: Critical review

In this crucial act, Shakespeare recalls Caesar's first entrance, as he presents him proceeding confidently towards the Senate House. He meets the Soothsayer, whose quiet reply to Caesar's challenge is no longer 'shriller than all the music', but ominous. Artemidorus' written warning is thrust aside by Caesar with a gesture that vindicates Calpurnia's 'Alas, my lord, / Your wisdom is consumed in confidence.' Shakespeare heightens suspense by introducing Popillius Lena's use of the word 'enterprise' in his passing comment to Cassius. There is a last-minute fear that the plans to kill Caesar are known.

Caesar prepares for the normal Senate procedure, but the planned behaviour of the conspirators manoeuvres him into acting like the tyrant they are primed to kill. Surrounded by supplicants, Caesar takes refuge in inflexibility, an illuminating confirmation that it is Caesar's susceptibility to provocation, rather than his ambition, that ultimately plays into the hands of his killers.

The prophecy of the Soothsayer is fulfilled. The plans of the conspirators are successfully implemented. In a paroxysm of stabbing, the life of Caesar ends and, with it, the dramatised conflict between Caesar the private man, aware of his mortality, and Caesar the all-powerful public figure. Calpurnia's dream of Romans bathing their arms in Caesar's blood becomes a reality.

The killing of Caesar is followed by confusion and dismay in the streets of Rome, but the murderers seem intoxicated by the success of their action. Brutus and Cassius proclaim a new, free Rome. Caesar's blood has both a dramatically visual and a symbolic importance. In overruling Cassius' judgement, Brutus allows Antony to speak to the people of Rome over Caesar's body.

While Brutus appeals to his listeners' minds with an argument that balances Caesar's virtues against his dangerous 'ambition', Antony's oration effectively combines genuine grief with deliberate incitement.

Shakespeare sets the righteous indignation of the plebeians against their mindless killing of Cinna the poet, so throwing into question both Antony's perception of popular justice and Brutus' political idealism.

Act 4 Scene 1

In this scene Shakespeare presents a view of Mark Antony which intensifies his dramatic complexity. Naive in his early judgement of Cassius, genuinely grief-stricken over Caesar's death, and deliberately manipulative in rousing the plebeians against the conspirators, Antony is now revealed as a cold, unsparing politician. He, Octavius Caesar and Lepidus will later make up the Triumvirate, the three-man government that will rule the Roman Empire. Since Brutus and Cassius have fled, Antony, Octavius and Lepidus discuss the necessary purge that will rid Rome of those in old positions of influence who might oppose them. Neither friend nor family relative is to be spared. Lepidus agrees to the death sentence on his brother on condition that Antony's own nephew must die. Antony does not hesitate, placing a black mark beside the name: 'He shall not live – look, with a spot I damn him.'

Antony sends Lepidus to fetch Caesar's will, so that the inheritance left to the people of Rome might be reduced in order to pay the costs of setting up the new government. Shakespeare starkly contrasts Antony's use of the will here with his apparent regard for its generosity to the common people in Act 3 Scene 2. With Lepidus away, Antony seeks to persuade the young Octavius of Lepidus' unimportance:

> This is a slight, unmeritable man,
> Meet to be sent on errands; is it fit,
> The threefold world divided, he should stand
> One of the three to share it? *(lines 12–15)*

But Octavius reveals a shrewdness for which Antony is unprepared. He reminds Antony that he had earlier accepted Lepidus' presence and his advice about who should be placed on the death list. Antony is unable to leave the issue aside. With some condescension, he hints at Octavius' inexperience and compares Lepidus to a pack animal fit to be used for burdensome work and then put out to 'graze' on common land. Octavius' brief response is non-committal, but he observes that Lepidus is 'a tried and valiant soldier'.

Antony seems intent on disparaging Lepidus. He continues at some length to dismiss him as one who has no mind of his own:

He must be taught and trained and bid go forth,
A barren-spirited fellow, one that feeds
On objects, arts, and imitations,
Which, out of use and staled by other men,
Begin his fashion. *(lines 35–9)*

Why is Antony so bent on destroying Lepidus' credibility? Does he imagine that with Lepidus sidelined to a mere messenger, he can bring his experience to bear on the young Octavius and so control him? Plutarch records that 'Antonius at the first made no reckoning of [Octavius], because he was very young; and said he lacked wit and good friends to advise him'. Whatever Antony's motives, he recognises the need to prepare an alliance against the military threat posed by the gathering forces under Brutus and Cassius. Octavius acknowledges their position with unmistakable realism:

Let us do so, for we are at the stake
And bayed about with many enemies,
And some that smile have in their hearts, I fear,
Millions of mischiefs. *(lines 48–51)*

Act 4 Scene 2

The sense of mistrust between Brutus and Cassius which is evident from the opening of this scene was suggested to Shakespeare by what he had read in Plutarch:

Now as it commonly happeneth in great affairs between two
persons, both of them having many friends and so many
captains under them, there ran tales and complaints betwixt
them.

Brutus confronts Pindarus and tells him that Cassius 'Hath given me some worthy cause to wish / Things done undone'. This, says Brutus, is either a result of Cassius' own changed feelings or of the malicious fabrications of subordinate officers. Notwithstanding Pindarus' assurance that Cassius comes to meet Brutus 'Such as he is, full of regard and honour', Brutus takes Lucilius aside and learns that Cassius' reception was courteous, but less friendly than usual. Accordingly, Brutus suspects that Cassius has become 'A hot friend cooling', and doubts his continuing commitment and reliability:

> But hollow men, like horses hot at hand,
> Make gallant show and promise of their mettle.
> But when they should endure the bloody spur
> They fall their crests, and like deceitful jades
> Sink in the trial. *(lines 23–7)*

On arrival, Cassius immediately accuses Brutus of having deceived him. So rashly does Cassius override Brutus' protestation of innocence that Brutus sees the need to conceal their quarrel from the watching soldiers, and they withdraw into Brutus' tent.

Act 4 Scene 3

The quarrel between Brutus and Cassius breaks like a storm in this scene. Cassius accuses Brutus of maligning an officer (Lucius Pella) for accepting bribes from the Sardians, and then disregarding Cassius' letter of defence. Brutus says Cassius has a reputation for 'an itching palm', a tendency to use his position to make money out of appointing undeserving men to privileged positions in return for gold. Cassius answers that had any man but Brutus spoken thus, he would be killed. Brutus reminds Cassius that Caesar was killed to further the cause of justice, not for the corrupt benefit of those who killed him:

> shall we now
> Contaminate our fingers with base bribes
> And sell the mighty space of our large honours
> For so much trash as may be graspèd thus? *(lines 23–6)*

Cassius' anger prompts him to claim that he is a soldier of more experience than Brutus, 'abler than yourself / To make conditions'. His words provoke Brutus, who shifts the focus of the quarrel to Cassius' petulance, confronting him with 'Must I stand and crouch / Under your testy humour?' He then punctures Cassius' self-importance by declaring his ill-temper amusing rather than fearsome. It is not a remark that Cassius is likely to enjoy. He has earlier revealed a tendency to take himself seriously (see Act 1 Scene 2, lines 72–8). Brutus taunts him about his boast of being 'a better soldier' and asks for evidence. Cassius denies the boast. When Cassius claims that Caesar would not have dared so to rouse him, Brutus retorts that Cassius would not have dared so to provoke Caesar. Unafraid of this new flare of angry menace from Cassius, Brutus gets to the nub of his own indignation:

> I did send to you
> For certain sums of gold, which you denied me,
> For I can raise no money by vile means.　　　*(lines 69–71)*

Not only is the issue one of the distribution of money, but at the centre is Brutus' sense that his own scrupulous honesty leaves him at a grave disadvantage. Short of resources and unable to pay his army, he resents the reports of Cassius' growing wealth received from bribes. In this it is evident that Shakespeare is following Plutarch, who records that

> Brutus prayed Cassius to let him have some part of his money,
> whereof he had great store . . . Cassius' friends hindered this
> request, and earnestly dissuaded him from it, persuading him
> that it was no reason that Brutus should have the money
> which Cassius hath gotten together by sparing and levied with
> great evil will of the people their subjects.

However, Shakespeare has not merely used Plutarch as a basis for the quarrel itself, but he has placed the centre of the dispute in the character differences of the two men. Brutus' directness throws Cassius on to the defensive. He first blames the messenger, claiming, 'He was but a fool that brought / My answer back', and then accuses Brutus of exaggerating his lapses. Finally he plays dramatically for sympathy, inviting both Brutus and Octavius to 'Revenge yourselves alone on Cassius'. He complains that he is hated by Brutus, whom he loves, is scrutinised like a slave, and that all his faults have been noted only to be used against him later:

> There is my dagger
> And here my naked breast: within, a heart
> Dearer than Pluto's mine, richer than gold.
> If that thou beest a Roman take it forth,
> I that denied thee gold will give my heart　　　*(lines 100–4)*

Cassius' revelation of his radical dependence on the friendship of Brutus, and the reconciliation that follows – initiated by Brutus – echo their first meeting in the play. As he had done on the earlier occasion, Brutus disarmingly admits shortcomings in himself and so restores the friendship. Shakespeare amplifies Cassius' psychological complexity, both in his compulsive need for Brutus' approval and in his acknowledgement of his mother's influence on his early years:

CASSIUS	O Brutus!
BRUTUS	What's the matter?
CASSIUS	Have not you love enough to bear with me

When that rash humour which my mother gave me
       Makes me forgetful?   *(lines 118–21)*

A poet, concerned at the dissent between the two generals, insists on seeing them. While Cassius finds the poet's intervention amusing, Brutus brusquely evicts him. This bizarre episode seems to have been prompted by Plutarch, who identifies

> One, Marcus Faonius [who] took upon himself to counterfeit a philosopher not with wisdom and discretion but with a certain bedlam and frantic motion, he would needs come into the chamber, though men offered to keep him out.

Plutarch further notes that Faonius, 'with a certain scoffing and mocking gesture', quoted lines from Homer. Why has Shakespeare introduced another poet here? Perhaps because his reception draws attention to the contrast in character between Brutus and Cassius. Brutus' uncharacteristic surliness prepares the theatre audience for his admission 'O Cassius, I am sick of many griefs', and his controlled distress at the news of Portia's death. Perhaps this poet episode is yet another ironic exploration of the relationship between words and action. The plebeians were moved against the conspirators by Antony's words – which Brutus did not stay to hear – and now Brutus dismisses the poet, and all poets, with 'What should the wars do with these jigging fools?'

In the final touches of reconciliation, Brutus tells Cassius that Portia, driven to distraction by the news of Octavius and Antony advancing to engage the armies of Brutus and Cassius, has 'swallowed fire' and so killed herself. Wine once more cements the friendship of Brutus and Cassius, just as it had earlier brought together the conspirators on the morning of Caesar's death.

Titinius and Messala bring news from Rome. The Triumvirate has executed a hundred senators, including Cicero. The army under Antony and Octavius is marching towards Philippi. Messala reports this to Brutus, unaware that he has heard of Portia's death, and is surprised but impressed that Brutus seems unaffected and impatient to propose that they march to engage Antony and Octavius at Philippi. Cassius is opposed to this tactic. He reasons sensibly that they would do better to wait for the opposing army to exhaust its energy in locating them:

> 'Tis better that the enemy seek us,
> So shall he waste his means, weary his soldiers,
> Doing himself offence, whilst we, lying still,
> Are full of rest, defence, and nimbleness.　　*(lines 199–202)*

Brutus dismisses Cassius' argument with a confident assertion of his own better judgement: 'Good reasons must of force give place to better'. He maintains that Antony and Octavius will get active support from the people living ''twixt Philippi and this ground'. These indigenous people will be willing recruits, swelling the number of the advancing army. It would be better, therefore, to pre-empt this threat and confront Antony and Octavius at Philippi. Brutus feels that a crucial moment has arrived, and in a memorable and extended image, urges that he and Cassius must seize the initiative:

> There is a tide in the affairs of men
> Which, taken at the flood, leads on to fortune;
> Omitted, all the voyage of their life
> Is bound in shallows and in miseries.
> On such a full sea are we now afloat,
> And we must take the current when it serves
> Or lose our ventures.　　*(lines 218–24)*

As in his earlier judgement of Antony, Brutus rashly overrules Cassius' caution. Despite misgivings, Cassius acknowledges that further argument is futile. He seems resigned to accepting Brutus' decision. Perhaps the rescued friendship is most important to him:

> O my dear brother!
> This was an ill beginning of the night.
> Never come such division 'tween our souls!
> Let it not, Brutus. *(lines 233–6)*

Left to take some rest before advancing to Philippi, Brutus reveals the unselfish, sympathetic side of his nature that he had shown in his own home. He asks Lucius for his gown and for some music, but he is quick to observe with compassion the tiredness in Lucius' voice. Plutarch notes Brutus' fondness for reading, and Shakespeare incorporates this with the passing touch of delight as Brutus finds his mislaid book. The comment reveals, too, the informal and warm relationship that has grown between Brutus and Lucius.

While others sleep, Brutus prepares to read. He becomes aware of a change in the quality of the candlelight. Following Plutarch, and in line with an Elizabethan superstition, Shakespeare includes this detail of light changing in the presence of a supernatural presence. Plutarch records the appearance of a ghost which he does not identify. But Shakespeare's stage direction makes clear that 'this monstrous apparition' is indeed the spirit of Caesar. The moment has great dramatic potential, but modern scepticism makes convincing staging difficult. In Shakespeare's day, many people believed in the existence of ghosts, and Caesar's ghost would no doubt have been distinctly recognisable – either bloodied or triumphant – on the stage. Today, directors of the play often differ sharply in their view of whether the ghost should physically appear, or whether it should be suggested by voice-over and lighting effects not available in Shakespeare's theatre.

The ghost promises to revisit Brutus at Philippi, and the repeated echo in 'thou shalt see me at Philippi' and Brutus' echoing of the words 'see thee at Philippi' gives this moment an ominous prophetic ring. With the ghost's exit, the isolation of Brutus is intensified as he questions the others who have been asleep in his tent. None has shared his vision of Caesar's ghost. Unable to sleep, Brutus gives the order to begin the advance to Philippi.

Act 4: Critical review

Act 4 opens in an atmosphere of quiet deliberation. A new order for the government of Rome and its Empire is taking shape. Antony, Octavius and Lepidus sit together as the Triumvirate to plan the elimination of those who held influence in the former regime.

The development of Antony's character becomes increasingly enigmatic. The rhetorical power with which he roused the plebeians against the conspirators and the stature he gained as the righteous avenger have been displaced by less attractive qualities. His bargaining over names on the death list, his reallocation of the wealth bequeathed in Caesar's will and his disparagement of Lepidus suggest that Antony might cherish his own ambitions for political leadership. But the quiet shrewdness of Octavius' responses to Antony indicates that Octavius will become an astute and formidable political player. For the present, he recognises the priority of forming an effective alliance against the armies of Brutus and Cassius.

The subdued uneasiness between Octavius and Antony is both reflected and thrown into relief by the quarrel between Brutus and Cassius. Brutus accuses Cassius of amassing wealth through bribes, and of refusing to share the wealth he has collected. The violent dispute endangers their alliance, but Cassius' dependence on Brutus' friendship (established in their first meeting) opens the way for reconciliation. Cassius allows Brutus to overrule his judgement on battle tactics, and agrees to march to Philippi.

It becomes clear that the stability of Caesar's rule over Rome has given way, not to 'Peace, freedom, and liberty!' as Brutus had proclaimed, but to confusion and uncertainty. The quarrel between Brutus and Cassius, Portia's suicide, and the disagreement over how to engage the enemy reflect the earlier prophetic disturbances of the storm, the images in the sky and Calpurnia's dream. With the killing of Caesar, order in the world has begun to disintegrate. The growing dissonance finds a trace in Lucius' 'The strings, my lord, are false' as he fails to play music to Brutus. The visitation of Caesar's ghost indicates the continuing influence of Caesar's spirit, and casts a dark shadow over the fortune of Brutus.

Act 5 Scene 1

This scene is set at Philippi, where the issue of who will rule the Roman Empire – the Triumvirate or the Republicans under Brutus and Cassius – will be settled. The dissension between Brutus and Cassius in the previous scene has its reflection in the exchanges between Octavius and Antony. Octavius observes that Antony's prediction of the opposing army's reluctance to enter into battle proves wrong. Antony, with some irritation, maintains that the enemy's advance is a mere tactic 'To fasten in our thoughts that they have courage. / But 'tis not so.' Octavius is vindicated by the messenger, who reports the rapid and bold approach of the enemy and urges Octavius and Antony that there is no time to lose.

Octavius overrules Antony's battle strategy and his claim to fight on the right-hand line of battle: 'Upon the right hand I, keep thou the left.' The young Octavius asserts himself with an unruffled firmness which unsettles Antony. To Antony's challenge, 'Why do you cross me in this exigent?' Octavius denies any deliberate provocation, but confronts Antony with a cold, fearless intention to question his judgement in the future.

In the parley which precedes the armed battle, the four generals meet to exchange taunts and accusations. Brutus' opening question is provocative: 'Words before blows; is it so, countrymen?' It revives a theme that has run through the play – the relation of words to actions. Antony reminds Brutus of the stark contrast between his idealistic words and 'the hole you made in Caesar's heart'. Cassius says that Antony's 'blows are yet unknown', but his sweet words of professed friendship after Caesar's death were like the honey stolen from the famous Hybla bees. The argument becomes more heated as Antony, Brutus and Cassius trade insults. In four sneering similes Antony bitterly scorns the conspirators:

> You showed your teeth like apes and fawned like hounds,
> And bowed like bondmen, kissing Caesar's feet,
> Whilst damnèd Casca, like a cur, behind
> Struck Caesar on the neck.   *(lines 41–4)*

Though Brutus says nothing, his reaction on the stage to this repugnant description will probably be strong, for he had once been primarily concerned with the style of Caesar's assassination ('Let's carve him as a dish fit for the gods'). Cassius, in the passion of the moment, turns on Brutus, reminding him that he had once recommended killing Antony as well as Caesar. By contrast, Octavius' intervention is noticeably cool and unerring in its aim:

> Look,
> I draw a sword against conspirators;
> When think you that the sword goes up again?
> Never, till Caesar's three and thirty wounds
> Be well avenged, or till another Caesar
> Have added slaughter to the sword of traitors.   *(lines 50–5)*

Brutus resents the implication that he is a traitor and declares that any traitors present would have come with Octavius. The hostility between them is undisguised as Octavius coldly asserts that he was born for better things than 'to die on Brutus' sword'. It is a retort that forces both Brutus and Cassius back onto desperate defence. They both claim that he is too young and inexperienced to understand, or to merit, so honourable a death.

Have Antony, Brutus and Cassius underestimated Octavius? He is indeed young, but he has shown himself to be controlled in his reactions, intelligent in his judgements, unconcerned about criticism and able to impose a natural authority. With a singleness of purpose he ignores Brutus' condescension and Cassius' description of him as 'A peevish schoolboy'. He thrusts home his moral advantage on the conspirators, insisting that they are 'traitors' and challenges them to prepare for battle.

There is no such confidence in the mind of Cassius, who seems to resign himself to an outcome which will be decided by Fortune. He confides to Messala that it is his birthday, and that like Pompey before him, he now has no option but to hazard the freedom they strove to give Rome upon the result of this one battle. Shakespeare draws on Plutarch in giving detail to Cassius' reflections. Plutarch records Cassius' change from following an Epicurean philosophy (which saw the gods as indifferent to the fate of humankind) to a superstitious belief in omens from the natural world. Cassius now sees a fearful symbolism in the carrion-eating birds that have replaced the eagles that followed their army:

ravens, crows, and kites
Fly o'er our heads and downward look on us
As we were sickly prey. Their shadows seem
A canopy most fatal under which
Our army lies, ready to give up the ghost.   *(lines 84–8)*

By the time Brutus returns from his discussion with Lucilius, Cassius has recovered his spirits. He greets Brutus brightly, but prepares him for defeat. Though he hopes the gods 'today stand friendly' allowing them to survive the battle and savour their friendship, the future is uncertain. He asks Brutus what he intends to do if they lose the battle. Brutus (who had once openly disapproved of Cato's suicide) maintains that he remains opposed to self-destruction as a remedy:

But I do find it cowardly and vile,
For fear of what might fall, so to prevent
The time of life   *(lines 103–5)*

The only alternative, Cassius reminds him, is to be led as a humiliated captive through the streets of Rome. Brutus recoils from this prospect and agrees that 'this same day / Must end that work the Ides of March begun'. In taking his farewell from Cassius, and in Cassius' repetition of the words, there is implicit agreement that they will take their own lives rather than accept defeat.

Act 5 Scene 2
In this short scene Brutus believes he can take advantage of what he perceives as a 'cold demeanour', a reluctance to fight, in the battle wing commanded by Octavius. He commits his legions to a 'sudden push', which he trusts will throw the enemy off balance. Messala obeys his general's orders without question, but in leaving Brutus with these few lines, Shakespeare has heightened the suspense, because Brutus' judgement on every crucial issue thus far has been seriously flawed.

Act 5 Scene 3
Cassius with dismay sees his soldiers fly in retreat. He tells his officer, Titinius, that in an effort to stem the flight he killed his own standard bearer, who was about to flee. Titinius explains that Brutus launched

his attack too early and with too little caution. His army lost its discipline and fell to looting the fallen enemy in retreat. This left the Republican army's flank exposed, allowing Antony's army to cut Cassius off from his base and advance upon his camp. Pindarus confirms Titinius' account and urges Cassius to 'Fly further off' to avoid being captured by Antony. Cassius, seeing his burning tents, sends Titinius with all speed to identify the soldiers in the distance.

Cassius, who once made much of Caesar's physical vulnerability, now reveals a weakness of his own, admitting he suffers from poor eyesight. He sends Pindarus to a higher point to report Titinius' fate. But Cassius seems to be in the process of accepting an internal defeat. He recognises this anniversary of his birth as his final day:

> This day I breathèd first, time is come round
> And where I did begin there shall I end:
> My life is run his compass.   *(lines 23–5)*

As if to justify Cassius' psychological surrender, Pindarus reports that Titinius has been surrounded, pursued and finally captured by horsemen who 'shout for joy'. This news resolves Cassius' mind on suicide as the only course now left to him as a noble Roman (see page 77). Reproaching himself for cowardice, he orders Pindarus to kill him in return for his freedom:

> Now be a freeman, and with this good sword,
> That ran through Caesar's bowels, search this bosom.
>   *(lines 41–2)*

Plutarch observed that when on military ventures Cassius was constantly accompanied by Pindarus 'whom he reserved ever for such a pinch'. With his last words, Cassius acknowledges that the sword's history has made him ultimately a victim of Caesar's revenge:

> Caesar, thou art revenged
> Even with the sword that killed thee.   *(lines 45–6)*

Pindarus, torn between guilt for killing his master and happiness at gaining his freedom, flees 'Where never Roman shall take note of him'. On the stage, the action usually flows swiftly from episode to episode, but here many productions pause briefly to present a still moment in which the audience can concentrate their full attention on the sight of Cassius' lifeless body. Messala enters with Titinius to reveal that Brutus' attack on Octavius' force appears to have been a surprising success, though Cassius' legions have paid the price, being scattered by Antony. Their reaction on seeing the body throws a new light on Cassius' character. Titinius' lament reveals that despite the bitterness with which Cassius had sought to belittle Caesar, he could inspire affection and admiration in others:

> O setting sun,
> As in thy red rays thou dost sink to night,
> So in his red blood Cassius' day is set.
> The sun of Rome is set.   *(lines 60–3)*

Yet both Titinius and Messala recognise that Cassius was driven to his end by an essential pessimism, by 'Mistrust of good success'. Perhaps that lack of generosity was what led him to see only what he wanted to see in the character of Caesar. Messala grieves that error, born of a melancholy disposition, leads men to see things wrongly. He leaves to tell Brutus the terrible news of Cassius' death. Left alone with Cassius' dead body, Titinius reveals the errors in Pindarus' report of his apparent capture. Instead of being surrounded by enemies, he was greeted by friends, whose shouts were cries of welcome. He speaks a line which might be Cassius' epitaph: 'Alas, thou hast misconstrued everything.' He places on Cassius' brow the garland of victory sent by Brutus and determines on his own suicide, using Cassius' sword.

The part played by Cassius' sword gives it the dramatic power of a character in the play. It is introduced as his suicide dagger in Act 1 Scene 3. Later, it is one of the swords which stabs Caesar. In the confrontation in Brutus' tent, Cassius challenges Brutus to kill him with it. In the present scene, only moments earlier he obliges Pindarus to kill him with it, and now Titinius takes it up: 'Come, Cassius' sword, and find Titinius' heart.' Just as Cassius could not live believing he had sent Titinius to his death, so now Titinius, moved by guilt for Cassius' suicide, takes his own life. The Roman code of honour takes its toll.

Shakespeare keeps up the dramatic momentum and brings the theme of Roman honour to the foreground as Brutus and his officers find the bodies of both Cassius and Titinius. As Cassius had done, Brutus now acknowledges Caesar's invincible spirit:

> O Julius Caesar, thou art mighty yet,
> Thy spirit walks abroad and turns our swords
> In our own proper entrails. *(lines 94–6)*

That these words should be spoken by Brutus, who once had wished that the conspirators 'could come by Caesar's spirit / And not dismember Caesar!', is one more of the play's resounding ironies.

Brutus' control over his own emotions – shown earlier when he appeared to brush aside the news of Portia's suicide – reveals itself again. He pays the highest tribute to Cassius, 'The last of all the Romans' and promises that later he will find time to mourn appropriately. But, mindful of his responsibilities as military commander, Brutus instructs that Cassius' body be sent to the island of Thasos so that the funeral will not demoralise his soldiers. As he had done in deciding to march to Philippi, Brutus hides his grief behind impulsive action:

> 'Tis three o'clock, and, Romans, yet ere night
> We shall try fortune in a second fight. *(lines 109–10)*

Act 5 Scene 4

This is the only scene that calls for a staged fight, with one character being killed and one taken prisoner. It reflects a less serious, less consequential aspect of the battle. Except for the opening line spoken by Brutus, the action is carried by young men keener on glamorous adventure and daring individual bravado than on overall military outcomes. In performance, the action, freed from political consequences, will depend for its effect on convincing energy and virtuoso athletic manoeuvres. Shakespeare no doubt had in mind young swashbucklers who swaggered about the streets of London in his day, drawing attention to themselves and to their swords.

Young Cato's boastful challenge, 'I am the son of Marcus Cato, ho!', only results in his being killed by Antony's soldiers. Lucilius seems to take his cue from Cato, proclaiming that he is Brutus, and challenging the soldiers to kill him. Believing him indeed to be Brutus, they take him prisoner (perhaps hoping for a noble prisoner's

ransom) and deliver him to Antony. Youthfully defiant, Lucilius
confronts Antony:

> I dare assure thee that no enemy
> Shall ever take alive the noble Brutus.   *(lines 21–2)*

Antony responds with the magnanimity of one who knows he is a
victor. He knows that Lucilius is not Brutus and perhaps he
recognises in Lucilius an affinity with his own audacious recklessness:
'I had rather have / Such men my friends than enemies.'

Act 5 Scene 5

After the brief but violent action of Scene 4, the dramatic climate
changes. The Republican army has been defeated. Brutus sits among
rocks near the battlefield. He is surrounded with followers who appear
here for the first time. Brutus has obviously decided on suicide, and
he whispers first to Clitus, then to Dardanius his decision to kill
himself. Both decline to help him, and Brutus makes a longer appeal
to his former schoolfriend, Volumnius. He confides that Caesar's
ghost has appeared twice to him, latterly, as the ghost had promised,
'this last night here in Philippi fields'. For Brutus, this indicates that
'my hour is come', but he cannot convince Volumnius of his certainty,
nor will Volumnius hold his sword whilst Brutus runs upon it: 'That's
not an office for a friend, my lord.'

Shakespeare intensifies Brutus' isolation as the alarums sound
progressively closer, indicating the inexorable advance of Antony and
Octavius. Clitus' 'Fly, fly, my lord, there is no tarrying here', carries
the plain meaning of self-preservation for him. But for Brutus, and for
an Elizabethan audience, 'tarrying here' means postponing his own
death. Shakespeare would have been mindful of Plutarch, who noted
Brutus' response: 'We must fly indeed . . . but it must be with our
hands not with our feet.' Brutus is resolved:

> I shall have glory by this losing day
> More than Octavius and Mark Antony
> By this vile conquest shall attain unto.   *(lines 36–8)*

Line 38 makes it clear that Brutus holds fast to his original
justification for killing Caesar in order to free Rome. The 'vile

conquest' by Antony and Octavius represents, for him, a new tyranny.

Now in his last minutes of life, Brutus feels the overpowering pull of sleep, so long denied him: 'Night hangs upon mine eyes, my bones would rest, / That have but laboured to attain this hour.' Anxious to send Clitus, Dardanius and Volumnius away, Brutus lies to them, 'Hence! I will follow.' Only Strato, who has 'been all this while asleep' (so suggesting another motif reminiscent of Lucius) remains with him. Strato agrees to assist Brutus' suicide and holds the sword that gave the final stab to Caesar. Brutus runs on the sword and, as Cassius had, in his last words unknowingly acknowledges what Antony had prophesied, 'Caesar's spirit, ranging for revenge':

> Caesar, now be still,
> I killed not thee with half so good a will.   *(lines 50–1)*

Antony enters with Octavius and the victorious army, and in his final lines, Antony identifies qualities that afford Brutus a claim to tragic stature. Of all the conspirators, he was 'the noblest Roman' because he was moved by a genuine belief in the good of Rome. He was by nature noble and generous, and the elements of his personality were so balanced

> that Nature might stand up
> And say to all the world, 'This was a man!'   *(lines 74–5)*

The closing lines of the play show Octavius to have asserted his leadership. His decision to pardon and take into his service 'All that served Brutus' is made independently and is undisputed by Antony. Like Julius Caesar, who had been magnanimous in showing clemency to Brutus and Cassius (both former followers of the defeated Pompey) he risks the later disaffection of those he spares. Yet Octavius' perceptive and calculating intelligence suggests that he now stands as the most powerful man on the political landscape of the Roman Empire. Productions often end by highlighting the final irony of the play. The work of the conspirators in removing Julius Caesar from his position is ultimately overtaken by the imposition of a new order. What lies ahead is a more subtle but ruthless despotism.

Act 5: Critical review

The dissension between Brutus and Cassius is now reflected in the exchanges between Octavius and Antony. Judging the enemy tactics differently from Antony, the young Octavius overrules Antony. In the parley that follows, Shakespeare has given Antony lines that strip all dignity from the conspirators' action in killing Caesar: 'You showed your teeth like apes and fawned like hounds'. In Octavius' strong, fearless challenge to Brutus and Cassius, Shakespeare seems to prepare the stage for a new avenger, whose sword will not be sheathed 'till Caesar's three and thirty wounds / Be well avenged'.

Cassius sees his life as having come full circle. As he prepares Brutus for defeat he begins to define the atmosphere of introspective dejection that will be a determining factor in their humiliation. Cassius, whose judgement has been sound both in the planning of the conspiracy and in military tactics, finally comes to the mistaken conclusion that Titinius has been captured and, in consequence, persuades Pindarus to assist in his suicide. In bringing Titinius back to discover Cassius' body, and in including Titinius' distress and suicide, Shakespeare bestows on Cassius the distinction of being held in affection by those who served him.

The suicides of Cassius and Titinius darken the shadow that now hangs over the final hours of Brutus' life. As he has done before, Brutus seeks relief from his unquiet mind in action. He leads Cato and Lucilius into a final skirmish, in which they are defeated.

The final scene is set in what editors describe as 'A rocky place'. In this place, imaginatively and scenically remote from the city of Rome, the dramatic action is powerfully contrasted. On the one hand, there is the hurried retreat of Brutus' remaining soldiers; on the other, the unsuccessful attempts of Brutus to enlist help with his suicide, and so to find the 'rest' which has eluded him through the action of the play.

Antony is left to capture the essence that affords Brutus the claim to tragic stature. But in giving Octavius the final authority in the play, Shakespeare sets the stage for the conflict between Antony and Octavius that he would dramatise later in *Antony and Cleopatra*.

Contexts

This section identifies the contexts from which *Julius Caesar* emerged: the wide range of different influences which fostered the creativity of Shakespeare as he wrote the play. These contexts ensured that *Julius Caesar* is full of all kinds of reminders of everyday life, and the familiar knowledge, assumptions, beliefs and values of Elizabethan England.

What did Shakespeare write?

Scholars agree that *Julius Caesar* was written in 1599, and that it was first performed in the same year on the stage of The Globe Theatre on London's Bankside. What was the play that Shakespeare wrote and his Globe audiences heard? No one knows for certain, because the original acting script has not survived, nor have any handwritten amendments he might subsequently have made. *Julius Caesar* was not printed until it appeared as one of 36 plays in the First Folio, published in 1623. All later editions take their textual authority from the First Folio. This Guide follows the New Cambridge edition of the play (also used in Cambridge School Shakespeare), which is based on the acknowledged authoritative text printed with striking clarity and precision in the First Folio of 1623.

What did Shakespeare read?

This section considers Shakespeare's sources and identifies the stories and dramatic conventions that fired Shakespeare's imagination as he wrote *Julius Caesar*.

The events that led up to the conspiracy and the assassination of Caesar occupied the public mind long before Shakespeare gave them dramatic life. Classical opinions on the personality of Caesar agreed on the paradoxical nature of the man. On the one hand, he emerged as a military tactician of great skill, a charismatic leader, a telling orator and a man of energy and physical toughness. He was also known to be generous in his dealings with friends and soldiers who served under him, moderate in his lifestyle and often compassionate in his judgements of others. His detractors, on the other hand, saw him as ruthless, calculating, sexually voracious and driven by ambition. While some considered his murder justified, most commentators condemned it as senseless and born of unworthy motives. These two conflicting views of Caesar gave rise to a traditional ambivalence in trying to assess with fairness and balance the character, motives and achievements of the tireless campaigner under whose legions the Roman Empire had spread so far.

For the story of the play Shakespeare turned to a text he had probably studied at school: Plutarch's *The Lives of the Noble Grecians and Romans*, translated from Greek into French by James Amyot, from French into English by Thomas North in 1579 and reprinted in 1595. Plutarch wrote his *Lives* some 150 years after Caesar's death, and what made this biographical narrative so attractive as potential drama was Plutarch's lively interest in the complexity of human nature. What he offered was a rich weave of personal detail, an appreciation of the risks which leaders take in making major decisions, and an appraisal of characters' motives. In the words of the scholar M H Shackford, Plutarch gave

> whatever seemed appropriate for explanation and interpretation of his hero. The little homely citations of mere gossip, the accounts of venturesome exploits stirring to the reader's imagination, the frequent parentheses, the constant bias towards ethical judgements, have their own integrity as parts of a method of portraiture which has delighted students of human motives, reasonings, and deeds.

Plutarch's interest in eminent leaders who made decisions with confidence, but who were vulnerable because of their own failings, has about it the ring of Greek drama. In *Julius Caesar*, some essential features of Aristotelian tragedy are found: the arrogant pride of Caesar, ominously darkened by ironies which allow the audience an awareness of approaching disaster, to which the hero–victim is blind; crucial reversals of fortune; consequences which engulf the whole community and which bring retribution upon Caesar's killers.

In order to give his play dramatic tension and to ensure its aesthetic unity, Shakespeare spent much energy in selecting from and shaping Plutarch's material in the *Lives* of Caesar, Brutus and Antony. Plutarch only briefly mentions the decision by the tribunes to strip decorations from Caesar's statues, but Shakespeare gives it prominence at the end of the opening scene, so enabling Cassius and Brutus to advance the plans for the conspiracy with some evidence of resistance to Caesar's growing power already established. Plutarch does not mention Calpurnia's presence at the Lupercal festival, while Shakespeare seizes the dramatic opportunity to include her, as a pretext for revealing Caesar's anxious hope for an heir. Plutarch records the Soothsayer's warning as coming after the Lupercal festival; Shakespeare times it to interrupt Caesar's triumphant procession, maximising its dramatic effect.

Drama is much concerned with the unfolding of character, and Shakespeare constantly sought the most effective means to dramatise character on the stage. For example, Plutarch mentions Caesar's suspicion of Cassius' 'pale looks', but the words 'lean and hungry', used to make Cassius distinctive, are Shakespeare's. Elsewhere, Plutarch records that Caesar's suspicion of 'these pale-visaged and carrion-lean people' is clearly directed at Brutus as well as Cassius. In limiting Caesar's doubts specifically to Cassius, Shakespeare is at pains to build a relationship of trust between Caesar and Brutus. Plutarch mentions Brutus' dedication to Republican ideals, his troubled spirit and his estrangement from Cassius because of rivalry for a civic position. Shakespeare transforms Brutus' attitude both to Cassius and to the conspiracy. In the play, Brutus is not self-seeking, and accordingly he takes the blame for neglecting the friendship. While Plutarch's Brutus is anxious about the hazardousness of the conspiracy, Shakespeare gives Brutus the more worthy concerns about its ethical and moral justification.

There is no basis in Plutarch for Brutus' long soliloquy in Act 2 Scene 1. In including it, Shakespeare not only saw the importance of deepening Brutus' character, but also was drawing on his earlier explorations of 'the divided self' in *Richard II* and *Henry IV*. Shakespeare developed the soliloquy as the most effective means to explore and display the inner conflicts intrinsic to his tragic heroes.

In Plutarch, the conspirators never debate the necessity of binding themselves to the conspiracy with an oath; Shakespeare adds psychological depth to Brutus' character by having Brutus strongly reject Cassius' urging that they should 'swear our resolution'. In Plutarch, Cicero is not approached to join the conspiracy because of his timidity, whereas in Shakespeare, Brutus bars him because he will not fall in with other people's suggestions. It is ironic that it is Brutus who refuses to heed Cassius' warnings about Antony's potential danger. In Plutarch, Antony is spared partly because Brutus insists his murder would be unethical, but largely because Brutus admires his qualities and thinks he will applaud the conspirators' apparent Republican ardour. Shakespeare gives dramatic expression to Brutus' scruples, but makes him responsible for the conspirators' disastrous misjudgement of Antony's potential to wreck the conspiracy.

Caesar's refusal of the crown is recorded in Plutarch, but Casca's sardonic report is Shakespeare's own embellishment. Shakespeare adds many touches to Plutarch's portrait of Caesar:

- the rapid oscillations from self-conscious, godlike posturing to his fleeting awareness of human frailty
- Caesar's warm geniality towards the killers he trusts as friends
- his admirable but fatal thrusting aside of Artemidorus' written warning: 'What touches us ourself shall be last served.' (Plutarch merely has Artemidorus jostled aside by the crowd of suitors.)

Shakespeare streamlines the sequence of events in Plutarch between the murder and Antony's funeral oration, to dramatise the contrast between Cassius' suspicion of Antony and Brutus' confident generosity. Shakespeare intensifies the complexity of Antony's tactics in his perilous situation. Antony is genuinely grieved by the brutal killing of Caesar, but he is also gauging the reactions of the conspirators and planning his next moves in such a way that will prompt Brutus to overrule Cassius' obvious distrust.

While Plutarch's description of the murder is gruesome in its detail, Shakespeare adds the horrific ceremony of the assassins bathing their arms in Caesar's blood in their attempt, however late, to bring a ritual dignity and style to their frenzied murder. It is ironic that Brutus, who earlier had overruled Cassius' conviction that Antony be killed with 'Our course will seem too bloody', now urges the conspirators to 'Stoop, Romans, stoop, / And let us bathe our hands in Caesar's blood'.

A final instance of Shakespeare's dramatic imagination is his repositioning of Brutus' knowledge of Portia's suicide. Plutarch mentions it almost as an afterthought, but in burdening Brutus with it before the quarrel with Cassius in Act 4 Scene 3, Shakespeare explains Brutus' unreasonable confrontation with Cassius, and so invites some sympathy for Brutus' deeply felt grief.

While Shakespeare heightened the tension between characters mentioned in Plutarch and gave their inter-relationships a dramatic priority, he also appreciated the need to adjust the pace of events to suit the demands of the stage. Accordingly, he cut Plutarch's intervening detail to build a new sequence, which makes Brutus' oration lead directly to Antony's. The dramatic action comes alive with the juxtaposition of Brutus' rational logic against Antony's deliberate arousal of the crowd.

Many of the details in Antony's oration are mentioned in Plutarch. The details in Caesar's will are there, but in Plutarch the will is read before Antony speaks, by an unidentified speaker. It is Shakespeare who has Antony read it to the crowd, and who arranges the timing of its revelation. Plutarch mentions the detail of Caesar's famous victory over the Nervii, evidence of Caesar's love for Brutus and Caesar's burying his face as Brutus prepares to stab him. But it is Shakespeare's dramatic imagination that shapes the sequence of Antony's delivery so that the cumulative effect of his speech unleashes the forces that will destroy the hopes of the conspiracy.

The biographical writings of Plutarch are essentially narrative sequences concentrating on personal characteristics and revealing detail, rather than making character relationships central as Shakespeare does. Shakespeare has developed his play and its dramatic tension from his capacity to communicate a sense of what the conspirators meant to each other, and to Caesar, and he to them and to Antony, and Brutus to Portia.

What was Shakespeare's England like?

The English history plays and *Julius Caesar*

It is clear from references and allusions in Shakespeare's earlier plays that the story of Caesar's assassination had preoccupied Shakespeare's imagination for nearly ten years before 1599. He had written a number of English history plays in the years preceding *Julius Caesar* (*Henry VI*, *Richard III* and *Richard II*, both parts of *Henry IV* and *Henry V*). Just as these plays reflected the expedient alliances and shifting loyalties that threatened the stability of the English monarchy, so *Julius Caesar* reveals the conspiratorial politics of Rome.

Shakespeare was reflecting ideas, attitudes and disaffected elements he observed in both the political and everyday life of London.

Politics

Caesar's Rome and Elizabethan England were transitional societies, caught up in a fundamental process of change. The change in England, from a medieval to a modern kingdom, involved difficult adjustments at all levels of society. There emerged a profound questioning of the position and power of the Church, and consequently of the traditional authority of the monarch. The Elizabethans viewed with intense interest – and with a lively division of opinion – the story of the rise and fall of Julius Caesar, for Caesar was a monarch in all but constitutional designation.

Caesar's assassination on the stage brought sharply to an audience's thoughts the attempts on the life of Queen Elizabeth. Just as Brutus and others worried about the unchecked growth of Caesar's power as a foreshadowing of tyranny, so there were deep concerns that Elizabeth's power was becoming conspicuously less accountable to any constitutional restraint. Like Caesar, Elizabeth too was increasingly subject to the infirmities of age. Like him, she was childless, and the lack of a legitimate heir to the throne fuelled the Elizabethans' great fear: political instability.

Shakespeare's *Julius Caesar* was both safe and intellectually provocative. On the one hand, it depicted mob violence as mindlessly destructive, a representation which would give comfort to a government that believed in the necessity of social control. On the other hand, it presented the struggle for the establishment of a Republican democracy to Elizabethans, who were in general committed to a belief in monarchy. Strict censorship laws in Elizabethan England would have prevented open public debate or any serious questioning of the powers of the English monarchy, but raising these questions in the remote historical setting of Rome could arouse thoughtful recognition in a safely oblique way. The fact that Brutus and Cassius failed in their revolutionary attempt would also have made the play seem suitably unthreatening to the English political establishment. Shakespeare's uncommitted view of Caesar reflects the divided views of the Elizabethans – and of Plutarch, who questioned whether Caesar was a tyrant or 'a merciful physician'. The assassination of Caesar – arguably the world's greatest empire builder

– could be seen by the Elizabethans, as it can today, either as a tragic act based on no substantial grounds, which destroyed the hopes for lasting political order and stability, or as a necessary and noble response to the rise of tyranny.

Rhetoric

The political dynamics of Ancient Rome made for captivating theatre, for the relationship between the governors and the governed was regulated through public oratory. The art of persuasive speaking and writing, known as rhetoric, was an essential accomplishment for those who aspired to take part in public life. Both in Rome and Elizabethan England, accomplished rhetoric assumed the mastery of five components for the successful composition and delivery of a public speech:

- finding the right material
- orderly arrangement of the material
- appropriate style and register of language
- memorisation
- effective delivery

Through the Middle Ages rhetoric was included as a highly significant part of the educational curriculum. A study of figurative language persisted right through the early modern period. Shakespeare and his educated contemporaries, then, would have shared a grasp of sophisticated and memorable language techniques, which Elizabethan politicians used as instruments to maintain power. In *Julius Caesar*, the longer speeches of Cassius, Brutus and Antony conspicuously demonstrate the art of rhetoric. They are filled with rhetorical devices, which make the language persuasively powerful and the situations vividly memorable. The public speeches to the plebeians demonstrate the use of rhetoric most clearly, but even the plans of the conspirators, or the dialogue between Antony and Octavius are often exercises in persuasion.

Three further features of the play would have enabled Elizabethans to recognise aspects of their own place and time within the setting of Shakespeare's drama. One was Rome's growing knowledge of the distant provinces of its Empire. The final battle for supremacy is fought not in the streets of Rome, but on the plains of Philippi in

Macedonia. The Roman Empire had been enlarged and subdued by military conquest. Elizabethan England was also gaining an awareness of the world beyond its shores, though not through conquest. Modern scholarship suggests that there was little imperial ambition among the Elizabethans. What fired the Elizabethan imagination about the wider world was a keen interest in travel literature (including writings by Hakluyt, Hawkins, Hariot and Sir Walter Ralegh between 1569 and 1596) and voyages made to explore trading opportunities.

A second recognisable feature for an Elizabethan audience was the nature of relationships between men. Elizabethan men formed friendships that were intense and profoundly loyal. The action of *Julius Caesar* is dramatised through the deep friendships between the main characters. That between the robust, athletic Antony and the ageing Caesar is established in the first act, as is the very different friendship between the stoical and idealistic Brutus and the power-fully driven Cassius. Both friendships forcefully shape the arching action of the play, which rises with the fortunes of the conspirators to the death of Caesar, and falls to military defeat and the suicides of Brutus and Cassius. The friendship between Caesar and Brutus places Brutus in a special category as traitor, not to a political cause as he wants it to seem, but to a personal and trusting friend whose unproven danger is that he *might* become a tyrant. While Caesar is a shrewd judge of men, it is one of the ironies in the play that he believes himself to be among friends when he drinks wine with his killers on the morning of his murder. The word 'love' is frequently used in connection with these friendships, and such a term would have been customary among Elizabethan men.

Finally, there was the question of how men saw their lives in relation to time and to history. To Elizabethans, the entire issue of time in the play would have been recognised as deeply significant. This interest in time, suggests Sigurd Burckhardt (see page 95), has its root in the Pope's reform of the traditional Christian calendar in 1582, a shift which became a contentious issue dividing Catholic and Protestant countries at the time. England, under the strongly Protestant Elizabeth, refused to accept a change that would make England subject to decisions and conditions approved by a Roman Catholic convocation on the continent of Europe. England therefore stuck to the old Julian calendar.

The growing agitation in England in favour of calendar reform prompted the publication of a number of popular almanacs which detailed the history of Julius Caesar and his own equally controversial institution of the Julian calendar in 45 BC. (The anti-Caesar lobby had protested that this was an arbitrary, tyrannical interference.) These almanacs also occasionally contained urgent appeals for the reform of the English calendar to bring it in line with the rest of Europe. By 1598, the discrepancy between the English Church calendar and that of Catholic Europe resulted in a five-week difference between the Catholic and Protestant celebrations of Easter. The insistence by Elizabeth and her government on adhering to the old Julian calendar (which was known to be mathematically erroneous) was seen by many in England as a national humiliation, and no less tyrannical than Caesar's imposition of his new calendar by decree in 45 BC.

This calendar debate gave late sixteenth-century Europe and Shakespeare's *Julius Caesar* (written and performed in 1599) a particular resonance with Caesar's Rome of 44 BC (see page 95). The pattern which emerges in Act 2 Scene 1 opens with attempts to clarify the time of day, the time of the month and the time of year. Brutus opens the scene with 'I cannot by the progress of the stars / Give guess how near to day.' When he later asks Lucius about the time of the month (which the First Folio text prints as 'Is not tomorrow, boy, the first of March') Lucius checks the calendar and tells Brutus that he is out by fourteen days: 'Sir, March is wasted fifteen days.' Later, the discussion between Casca, Decius and Cinna is about just where the sun will rise at this 'the youthful season of the year'. The uncertainties are about the time of day, the time of the month, the time of the year. Only when the last question of the assassination plan is settled does a clock strike. There were no clocks in Caesar's Rome, and many editors have considered the clock striking as an unfortunate anachronism (a staging detail out of the play's period). Later scholars have seen in the striking of the clock a significant detail, which an Elizabethan audience would have recognised as making the issue of time in the play resonant with that of their own period.

Tragedy

Julius Caesar can also be understood in the context of the Elizabethan appetite for revenge tragedy. Audiences flocked to such plays; it was a highly popular genre. A collection of tragedies based on Greek mythology by the Roman playwright, Seneca, was published in 1581. Seneca's impact on English playwrights, including Shakespeare, was profound. His tragedies of revenge prompted a spate of imitations in the 1580s and 1590s.

In the early 1590s Shakespeare had already written one revenge tragedy which depicted the excesses of imperial power: *Titus Andronicus*. The public demand for such plays partly explains why Shakespeare, responding to the likely box-office receipts, wrote *Julius Caesar* as one of the first plays to be staged in the newly completed Globe Theatre. In the First Folio, the play is placed with the tragedies, and although not described as a tragedy in the contents list, it is entitled *The Tragedy of Julius Caesar* above the printed text. Elements in the characterisation of Cassius resemble those of the traditional avenger. Partly because of his own sense of insignificance beside Caesar, Cassius sees the general subservience before the greatness of Caesar as dishonourable. He feels wronged by being 'A wretched creature' who must bow and scrape at Caesar's nod. There is a compulsive urge in Cassius to see the period as corrupted by Caesar and Rome's acceptance of him: 'Age, thou art shamed!' Yet, for Cassius, Caesar is 'but one only man' and therefore assailable:

> I had as lief not be as live to be
> In awe of such a thing as I myself.   *(Act 1 Scene 2, lines 95–6)*

In other respects, *Julius Caesar* inclines towards Aristotle's defining characteristics of classical Greek tragedy, particularly in showing a great man being brought low by a fatal error of judgement (*hamartia*). Caesar is an established great ruler of a vast, decisively conquered empire. He returns to Rome in triumph, but his ambition for power makes dangerous enemies. His calamitous fall is in part due to his pride and arrogance, combined with his own errors of judgement. Yet, as a tragedy, the play is unusual in dispensing with Caesar (after whom the play is named) early in Act 3 Scene 1, and in giving the deeper tragic development to Brutus. Shakespeare locates within him an agonising inner conflict and isolation. His soliloquy as he confronts the prospect of assassinating Caesar reflects both a depth of character and a moral dilemma. Indeed, one critical view suggests that Shakespeare began the play as the tragedy of Caesar and completed it as the tragedy of Brutus.

A particular feature of revenge tragedy is the use of the original murder weapon as the instrument of revenge. So, in *Julius Caesar*, Cassius acknowledges that Caesar's revenge is delivered 'Even with the sword that killed thee'. Ultimately it is the spirit of Caesar, resurrected through Mark Antony, that sets in motion the retribution that falls upon Brutus and Cassius and throws Rome into civil war. While *Julius Caesar* is not a conventional revenge tragedy, it nonetheless effectively mingles classical elements with those which take their roots from Senecan tragedy and which anticipate the Jacobean genre.

Marriage and the husband's authority

There are only two scenes in *Julius Caesar* which have domestic settings. Portia and Brutus are seen at home in Act 2 Scene 1, and Caesar and Calpurnia in Act 2 Scene 2. Since Shakespeare was not writing history, but a play to be performed before audiences of his time, it seems likely that these two marriages reflected the orthodox priorities and the tensions that were to be found in Elizabethan England. *The Elizabethan Homily on the State of Matrimony* was regularly read aloud in church. It ordered wives to obey their husbands, and instructed husbands that 'the woman is a frail vessel and thou art therefore made the ruler and head over her'.

The second scene of *Julius Caesar* opens with Caesar calling his wife's name as a single word, twice, and then ordering, rather than asking: 'Stand you directly in Antonio's way / When he doth run his course.' Calpurnia makes no protest, and the assumption is that she obeys without resentment. In his instruction to Antony, Caesar makes it clear that Calpurnia's failure to bear an heir is a major preoccupation, and that it is not he, but she who is responsible:

> for our elders say
> The barren, touchèd in this holy chase,
> Shake off their sterile curse.   *(Act 1 Scene 2, lines 7–9)*

Caesar's words reflect a similar anxiety felt by the Elizabethans. Queen Elizabeth was unmarried and childless, there was no clear heir to England's throne and the queen's increasing infirmity gave similar cause for concern to the Elizabethans (see page 69).

When in Act 2 Scene 2 Calpurnia pleads with Caesar not to venture forth to the Senate House (see pages 24–6), Caesar is resolute:

'Caesar shall forth', 'Yet Caesar shall go forth'. When the servant returns to report that the augurers 'would not have you to stir forth today', Caesar again insists: 'Caesar shall go forth'. Caesar only acknowledges the intensity of Calpurnia's concern when she absolves him of the responsibility for his own repressed uneasiness: 'Call it my fear / That keeps you in the house, and not your own.' Recognising that she can have no authority, her intervention is abject: 'Let me, upon my knee, prevail in this.' Caesar's acquiescence is quickly overturned by Decius' obsequious interpretation of Calpurnia's dream, so that Calpurnia is made the victim of Caesar's embarrassment. Dismissing the genuine feeling of his wife, Caesar is won over by crude flattery.

The marital relationship between Brutus and Portia is governed by the same Elizabethan conventions of patriarchal authority, but Shakespeare has altered its dynamics to reveal the different temperaments of the characters he has created. In coming upon Brutus after the conspirators leave in Act 2 Scene 1 (see pages 22–3), Portia does not confine her approach to pleading. Rather she confronts Brutus with the central substance of his marriage obligations as a husband. Brutus has abandoned the marital bed, has disrupted meals by leaving the table and has, with unseemly irritation, refused to share the burden of his mind. Portia will not be put off by Brutus' excuses of ill health, and her lines (268–75) suggest the genuinely affectionate and loving relationship that undoubtedly also existed between many Elizabethan husbands and wives. But the following words are a stinging challenge, and they reveal another aspect of Elizabethan London:

> Dwell I but in the suburbs
> Of your good pleasure? If it be no more
> Portia is Brutus' harlot, not his wife.
>
> *(Act 2 Scene 1, lines 285–7)*

Close to Shakespeare's Globe Theatre was the notorious brothel district of London's South Bank (referred to as the 'suburbs'), as the audience would be well aware. It is possible that on the Globe stage, Portia accompanied her remark with a gesture in the direction of the brothel quarter outside the theatre walls to reinforce its topicality, bringing Brutus to his deeply pained response, 'You are my true and honourable wife'. Unlike Calpurnia's plea to Caesar, Portia's challenge to Brutus shames him into the promise, even while Ligarius knocks on the door, to share with her the troubles that beset him:

> And by and by thy bosom shall partake
> The secrets of my heart.
> All my engagements I will construe to thee,
> All the charactery of my sad brows.   *(Act 2 Scene 1, lines 305–8)*

Portia's agitated excitement in Act 2 Scene 4 (see page 29) suggests that Brutus has been as good as his word.

The plague, sickness and disease

A variety of unpleasant, contagious and infectious diseases were common in Elizabethan England. Sexual diseases, known generally as 'the pox', were widespread and had severely damaging effects on the physical and mental health of successive generations. But the most feared and most prevalent disease that ravaged the cities was the bubonic plague. For all Londoners, the plague was a constant threat. Almost every member of a theatre audience in the late 1590s would know some friend, neighbour or family member who had fallen victim to the epidemics, which occurred all too frequently in England, disrupting normal life. Medical opinion of the time did not connect the disease with rats and fleas. The plague was thought to be spread by contagion from the air, or from contact with those who suffered from it. Consequently, the most immediate response to an outbreak of the disease was a closing of the theatres. Between 1593 and 1594, only five years before the first performance of *Julius Caesar*, a severe epidemic of the plague had closed all the theatres in London.

The location of The Globe, surrounded by brothels and prisons, and adjacent to St Thomas's Hospital, would also make its audiences and the authorities who licensed theatres especially anxious about the increased likelihood of infection. Murellus' 'fall upon your knees / Pray to the gods to intermit the plague' would have had an immediate relevance for London audiences at the play's inaugural performance at The Globe.

Julius Caesar is shot through with instances of sickness and infirmity. The relatively unsophisticated medical practices of both Caesar's and Shakespeare's times would have done little to remedy chronic suffering. Calpurnia's infertility, Caesar's deafness and his epilepsy, Brutus' insomnia, Ligarius' 'ague' which made him lean, Cassius' poor eyesight – are all details which Shakespeare has woven significantly into the body and consciousness of his characters, and which also act as reminders to Elizabethan audiences of their own physical susceptibilities.

Shakespeare reflects the Elizabethan concern with the question of how far the condition of the body reflected the state of the mind. Portia discounts Brutus' complaint, 'I am not well in health', and diagnoses 'some sick offence within your mind'. Ligarius, fired into action by joining the conspiracy declares, 'I here discard my sickness!' Sickness and health also have their thematic significance in both the condition of Rome and the limitations of character. Brutus describes the conspiracy as 'A piece of work that will make sick men whole', while Ligarius knowingly responds, 'But are not some whole that we must make sick?' Cassius' poor eyesight not only results in the error that prompts his suicide, but corresponds with his failure to see beyond his own personal hatred of Caesar. Shakespeare highlights the general sense of failing health which afflicts many of the characters by contrasting against it the enduring robustness of Antony.

Religion

The pre-Christian Roman setting of *Julius Caesar*, though seemingly far removed from the religious preoccupations of the Elizabethans, nonetheless raised compelling moral questions which were fiercely debated at the time. In presenting the suicides of Cassius and Brutus as honourable ways to die, Shakespeare was engaging the minds of his audience in a difficult topic. In the context of Ancient Rome these suicides were ennobling, but in the context of Christian Elizabethan England, they were not.

Caesar listens to the warning of the Soothsayer, but defies it and appeals to yet another set of pre-Christian religious practices. He sends to the priests and awaits 'their opinions of success'. When they, too, advise caution, he refuses to heed them, and ultimately assumes the superhuman quality of constancy, declaring himself the one man 'Unshaked of motion'. The force that is to dominate the post-Caesarean cosmos of the play becomes clearly identifiable in Antony's prophecy (Act 3 Scene 1, lines 262–75): 'Caesar's spirit, ranging for revenge, / With Ate by his side'. Both Cassius and Brutus acknowledge Caesar's spirit as the ultimate avenger (see pages 58, 62).

Yet despite the pre-Christian Roman setting, some critics have argued that there is an inescapable Christian resonance in the action. Steve Sohmer discusses in detail the interplay between the assassination of Caesar as Shakespeare depicts it and the betrayal and crucifixion of Christ. While some scholars have seen Caesar's tasting wine with his murderers as reminiscent of the Last Supper, Sohmer parallels it with Christ's first miracle, the turning of water into wine. At the subsequent wine-tasting at the marriage feast at Cana, Christ tells his mother, 'Mine hour is not yet come'. This event is narrated only in St John's Gospel 2, which, in the Elizabethan Church calendar, was also the reading scheduled for the Ides of March.

Sohmer's argument is both intriguing and plausible. The tantalising question that arises from it is about the nature of the relationship between St John's narrative and Shakespeare's inclusion of Caesar's wine-tasting gathering. Was Shakespeare using the Bible to confer a Christlike dimension to Caesar, or was he inviting his audience to 'speculate along the line that, like Caesar, Christ was a mortal man who claimed divine antecedents'? Many in Shakespeare's theatre audiences would no doubt have responded with recognition to the powerful symbols of sacrifice, blood, wine and betrayal on the morning of Caesar's murder. The unstable mix of personal, political and idealistic motives which are fused together and which make legitimate the killing of a victim would no doubt be similar, be the victim Christ or Caesar.

Death

The Elizabethans were profoundly preoccupied with death and decay. Insistent indications of death were the plague pits, mass graves containing unidentified corpses, which were located all around London and which produced the constant stench of decomposing flesh. The smell of putrefaction also leaked from tombs in churches, and rotting carcasses hanging from gibbets and city gates were a common sight. The closing lines of Antony's prophecy in Act 3 Scene 1 ('That this foul deed shall smell above the earth / With carrion men groaning for burial') would have recalled for Shakespeare's audiences vividly familiar experience.

Julius Caesar is a play infused with the idea and the physical fact of death. Casca reports that Flavius and Murellus have been 'put to silence'. Cassius tells Casca that he will stab himself if Caesar is

crowned, and that life 'Never lacks power to dismiss it
sees only one way of checking Caesar's growing power: 'I
his death.' The murder of Caesar can be staged as a prolc
stabbing. It is followed by the display of his body as Antony addresses
the crowd. The enraged mob cry 'Seek! Burn! Fire! Kill! / Slay! Let not
a traitor live!' The innocent poet, Cinna, is savagely murdered in a
frenzy. The Triumvirate sit together to decide on the many who are on
the list to die. Portia kills herself by swallowing fire. The ghost of
Caesar visits Brutus. Cassius persuades Pindarus to kill him.
Discovering the dead Cassius, Titinius kills himself. After failing to
persuade three of his friends to kill him, Brutus finally enlists the help
of Strato in his suicide.

The play's preoccupation with death is balanced by a growing
awareness of the spirit of Caesar asserting itself from beyond the
grave. The most concrete presentation of Caesar's posthumous power
is his will. The dead body of Caesar, displayed upon the stage and
revealed as Antony discourses upon it and holds up the cloak that
covered it, is not merely a visual reminder of the mortality of the flesh.
But, as Antony speaks over the body, he brings to life the spirit of
Caesar, the force which will transcend the corpse on the platform. The
body of Caesar can arguably be seen as becoming a kind of text, whose
marks and signs, writ large by the murderers, Antony interprets for
those who listen. Like a text, it will have the power to defeat mere
material decomposition, and will live to resonate through future
generations.

Language

Expressions from *Julius Caesar* have become universally known. Many phrases have passed into everyday speech: 'Beware the Ides of March', 'lend me your ears', '*Et tu Brute?*', 'There is a tide in the affairs of men', and many others.

But the language of the play is much more than a treasure house of quotations. It contains a wide variety of language registers. Simply listing a few types of language used can show its stylistic diversity:

- the language of authority used by the tribunes ('Hence! Home, you idle creatures, get you home!', Act 1 Scene 1, line 1) and by Caesar ('Thy brother by decree is banishèd', Act 3 Scene 1, line 44)
- witty and deliberate wordplay in the puns used by the plebeians: 'I am indeed, sir, a surgeon to old shoes: when they are in great danger I recover them.' (Act 1 Scene 1, lines 22–4)
- the language of abuse used by Murellus to the plebeians as he dehumanises them: 'You blocks, you stones, you worse than senseless things!' (Act 1 Scene 1, line 34)
- the arrogance of Caesar: 'Have I in conquest stretched mine arm so far / To be afeard to tell greybeards the truth?' (Act 2 Scene 2, lines 66–7)
- the ominous, blunt warning of the Soothsayer: 'Beware the Ides of March.' (Act 1 Scene 2, line 18)
- Antony's prophetic images of war and destruction: 'That mothers shall but smile when they behold / Their infants quartered with the hands of war' (Act 3 Scene 1, lines 267–8)
- the dry logic of Brutus' funeral oration: 'If then that friend demand why Brutus rose against Caesar, this is my answer: not that I loved Caesar less, but that I loved Rome more.' (Act 3 Scene 2, lines 18–20)
- the ecstatic cries of 'Peace, freedom, and liberty!' urged by Brutus (Act 3 Scene 1, line 110)
- the mob's shouting, 'Revenge! About! Seek! Burn! Fire! Kill!' (Act 3 Scene 2, line 195)

Many of these examples hint at the one dominant attribute of the language of *Julius Caesar*: the tenacity of its seeking to persuade. The critic Anne Barton has observed that 'Shakespeare constantly directs his audience's attention towards Rome as a city of orators and rhetoricians: a place where the art of persuasion was cultivated, for better or worse, to an extent unparalleled in any other society.' That persuasion is evident in a multitude of examples, most notably in the forum speeches of Brutus and Antony. It also occurs as self-persuasion, when Brutus, in soliloquy, seeks reasons to convince himself that the assassination of Caesar is justified. Shakespeare even portrays it silently in the play's final scene, as Brutus whispers to Clitus and Dardanius in unsuccessful attempts to persuade them to help him commit suicide.

Rhetoric uses a range of methods to make language more memorable, to leave phrases and sentences ringing in the minds of listeners or readers. One example is the use of the rhetorical question: a question that does not require an answer. It assumes that those who listen will answer it for themselves, but will reach the conclusion the speaker wants them to. Brutus uses rhetorical questions in his reading of Cassius' letter: 'Am I entreated / To speak and strike?' and to even greater effect in his funeral oration, as he persuades the listening plebeians of the necessity of Caesar's death: 'Who is here so vile that will not love his country?'

Antithesis

Antithesis is the opposition of words or phrases against each other, as in 'Set honour in one eye and death i'th'other' (Act 1 Scene 2, line 86); 'A man of such a feeble temper should / So get the start of the majestic world' (Act 1 Scene 2, lines 129–30). In these sentences, 'honour' and 'death' stand against each other; 'feeble' and 'majestic' are also antithetical. This setting of word against word is one of Shakespeare's favourite language devices. He uses it extensively in all his plays. Why? Because antithesis powerfully expresses conflict through its use of opposites, and conflict is the essence of all drama. To make his persuasion effective, Cassius uses antithesis consistently in his relentless reduction of Caesar: 'this man / Is now become a god'. In Antony's oration, antithesis is used to heighten dramatic contrast and show the rapidity of the change wrought by the killing of Caesar: 'But yesterday the word of Caesar might / Have stood against the world; now lies he there', with 'yesterday' opposed to 'now' and 'stood' to 'lies'. To Caesar's 'The Ides of March are come', the

Soothsayer replies, 'Ay, Caesar, but not gone.' 'Come' and 'gone' carry the ironic weight of the opposition.

In *Julius Caesar*, conflict occurs in many forms: the conspirators versus Caesar, sickness versus health, body versus spirit, idealism versus political opportunism, individual conscience versus mob destructiveness. It can be seen when the generous trust with which Brutus offers to receive Antony in 'With all kind love, good thoughts, and reverence' (Act 3 Scene 1, line 176) is contrasted with Cassius' astute recognition of Antony's danger. Antithesis intensifies the sense of conflict, and embodies its different forms. For example, Brutus' argument that Antony should be spared (Act 2 Scene 1, lines 162–83) contains at least 12 antitheses in 21 lines. They include: 'head'/'limbs', 'wrath in death' / 'envy afterwards', 'sacrificers'/'butchers', 'come by Caesar's spirit' / 'not dismember Caesar', 'kill him boldly' / 'but not wrathfully', 'carve him as a dish fit for the gods' / 'Not hew him as a carcass fit for hounds', 'masters'/'servants', 'Stir up' / 'seem to chide', 'purgers' / 'not murderers'. The cumulative effect of such antitheses suggests that the assassination can be carried out in two contrasting ways. Brutus seems to believe that if Caesar is killed in the right style, with the avoidance of cynical opportunism, the murder will have a respectable dignity. By piling the contrasts upon each other, he widens the gulf between a vicious killing, which would carry with it guilt, and a noble assassination that he hopes to make honourable.

Imagery

Although some critics have asserted that *Julius Caesar* contains few images (see page 92), the play in fact abounds in imagery: vivid words and phrases that help create the atmosphere of the play as they conjure up emotionally charged mental pictures in the imagination. Shakespeare seems to have thought in images, and the whole play richly demonstrates his unflagging and varied use of verbal illustration. One way to understand the dramatic effect of imagery is to see it as making abstract qualities concrete. When Brutus finds Lucius asleep, he wishes him the pleasure of 'the honey-heavy dew of slumber' (Act 2 Scene 1, line 230), so combining the heavy, slow flow and the sweetness of honey with the light, imperceptible condensation of dew. When Antony challenges those who have murdered Caesar to kill him without delay, he uses a vivid image which appeals to the senses of both sight and smell: 'Now, whilst your purpled hands do reek and smoke, / Fulfil your pleasure.'

Images carry powerful significance far deeper than their surface meanings. A striking succession of imagery emerges in Antony's prophecy over the dead body of Caesar, which works to its climax with:

> Cry havoc and let slip the dogs of war,
> That this foul deed shall smell above the earth
> With carrion men groaning for burial.
>
> *(Act 3 Scene 1, lines 273–5)*

When Antony speaks of 'the dogs of war', he is employing one of several animal images in the play. Animal imagery, widely used by Shakespeare in many of his plays, is not a dominant feature of *Julius Caesar*, but where it occurs it functions effectively, often revealing as much about the speaker as about the subject. Antony refers to Caesar as a 'brave hart', a 'deer' hunted in the forest. Cassius labels Caesar 'wolf' and 'lion' because the Romans behave like 'sheep' and 'hinds'. The Roman plebeians are 'bees', robbed by Antony's words of their honey. Antony's contempt for the conspirators is evident in his view of them as grinning 'like apes' and fawning 'like hounds'. He scorns Lepidus as an 'ass'.

Brutus' soliloquy (Act 2 Scene 1, lines 10–34) provides the most memorable of such animal images: 'It is the bright day that brings forth the adder'. The adder represents the hidden danger that lurks where it is least suspected, and so in Brutus' own train of thought such snake images emerge again as 'the serpent's egg'.

Shakespeare's imagery uses metaphor, simile or personification. All are comparisons which in effect substitute one thing (the image) for another (the thing described).

- A simile compares one thing to another using 'like' or 'as'. For example, Cassius describes Caesar's calling for water 'As a sick girl' when he was ill in Spain. Antony sees the murdered Caesar 'like a deer strucken by many princes', and prepares to prophesy over Caesar's wounds, 'Which like dumb mouths do ope their ruby lips'.
- A metaphor is also a comparison, suggesting that two dissimilar things are actually the same. When Brutus says 'lowliness is young ambition's ladder', an abstract human quality (lowliness) becomes

a familiar object one can touch and feel and see: a ladder with one end pointing upward. 'Ambition' becomes a young, keen climber (see the comments on personification below). To put it another way, a metaphor borrows one word or phrase to express another. For example, when Brutus says, 'Night hangs upon mine eyes, my bones would rest', 'night' stands for Brutus' tiredness, but it is given a heaviness – perhaps like a curtain – that pulls his eyelids closed. 'My bones would rest' is a metaphor insofar as it uses physical parts of the body to represent his own mind's desire.

• Personification turns all kinds of things into people, giving them human feelings or attributes. When Brutus says:

> O conspiracy,
> Sham'st thou to show thy dang'rous brow by night,
> When evils are most free?   (*Act 2 Scene 1, lines 77–9*)

he gives conspiracy human feelings (shame) and a human forehead (brow). When Antony shows the crowd Brutus' knife thrust through Caesar's cloak, he says the blood followed the withdrawal of Brutus' knife 'As rushing out of doors to be resolved / If Brutus so unkindly knocked or no', and so gives Caesar's blood the human quality of disbelief (for betrayal by Brutus was beyond the power of Caesar's imagination). Similarly, when Antony says of Brutus 'Nature might stand up / And say to all the world, "This was a man!"', Nature is given human stature, voice and authority of judgement.

Repetition

The play has structural repetitions which increase its dramatic intensity. For instance, in the domestic scenes (Act 2 Scenes 1 and 2), the intervention by the wives of Brutus and Caesar are important, but have no effect on the movement of the conspiracy. In both scenes, too, private domestic affairs are intruded upon by the conspirators. The quarrel between Brutus and Cassius in Act 4 Scene 3 is mirrored by that between Antony and Octavius in Act 5 Scene 1. But repetition is most apparent in the play's language, and is yet another rhetorical device. Different forms of language repetitions run through the play, contributing to its atmosphere, the creation of character, and the dramatic impact. One instance is Brutus' reading of the letter penned by Cassius. Parts of the letter catch Brutus' attention, and his repeating of them reveals the effectiveness of the tactic Cassius used to trick Brutus into joining the conspiracy. 'Rome' clearly resonates in Brutus' mind as he echoes the letter's cryptic reference; he seems possessed by it as he makes his promise to liberate the city (Act 2 Scene 1, lines 46–58). It is ironic that Brutus repeats the letter's accusation that he is sleeping ('Brutus, thou sleep'st. Awake'), for throughout the play indications of his insomnia recur.

Apart from familiar functional words ('the', 'and', etc.) the five lexical words most frequently repeated are 'Caesar' and 'Brutus' (each used over 100 times), 'good' (around 70 times) and 'men' and 'man' (each used over 50 times). The repeated use of the names points to the crucial relationship in the play between the protagonists, Caesar and Brutus. Repetition of 'good' reflects the constant attempt to ascribe a worthy motivation to action. Rome is manifestly a male-dominated society, though the play on 'man' and 'men' also implies questions about just how masculinity reveals itself.

Shakespeare's skill in using repetition to heighten theatrical effect and deepen emotional and imaginative significance is most evident in particular speeches. Repeated words, phrases, rhythms and sounds add intensity to the moment or episode. Repetition is much used in the first scene. Here, the piling up of rhetorical questions is a persuasive device first seen in Murellus' reprimand to the plebeians:

> And do you now put on your best attire?
> And do you now cull out a holiday?
> And do you now strew flowers in his way . . .?
>
> *(Act 1 Scene 1, lines 47–9)*

Repetition is a distinctive feature of Antony's irony in his funeral oration, as he plays with the word 'honourable', using it mockingly at least nine times to cast doubt on the integrity of Brutus and the conspirators. Antony is addressing the Roman plebeians, and his repeated use of 'honourable' ensures that it comes to mean its opposite in the minds of the listening crowd.

A different kind of repetition is found in Brutus' funeral oration, which is rich in restatement as a rhetorical device. His first three sentences have a similar structure, echoing the verb so that each sentence ends with the word or concept with which it began:

Romans, countrymen, and lovers, hear me for my cause, and
be silent that you may hear. Believe me for mine honour, and
have respect to mine honour that you may believe. Censure me
in your wisdom, and awake your senses that you may the
better judge.   *(Act 3 Scene 2, lines 13–16)*

A second kind of repetition emerges at lines 21–3. Here, Brutus
identifies four qualities in Caesar and describes his own response to
each. Immediately after this, Brutus repeats what he has just said in a
condensed form: 'There is tears for his love, joy for his fortune,
honour for his valour, and death for his ambition.' In his third
variation of repetition Brutus employs the rhetorical technique
foreshadowed in the opening scene. Brutus throws down three
questions: 'Who is here so base . . .?', 'Who is here so rude . . .?', 'Who
is here so vile . . .?' And to each of these rhetorical questions Brutus
presents the challenge 'If any, speak, for him have I offended.'

Occasionally, repetition will have its effect in a subtle echoing of an
idea that has emerged at an earlier point in the play. An example is
Antony's tantalising the crowd with Caesar's will: 'You are not wood,
you are not stones, but men' (Act 3 Scene 2, line 134), which recalls
and reverses Murellus' reprimand in the opening scene: 'You blocks,
you stones, you worse than senseless things!' (Act 1 Scene 1, line 34).

Lists

One of Shakespeare's favourite language methods is to accumulate
words or phrases rather like a list. He had learned the technique as a
schoolboy in Stratford-upon-Avon, and his skill in knowing how to use
lists dramatically and persuasively is evident in the many examples in
Julius Caesar. He intensifies and varies description, atmosphere and
argument as he 'piles up' item on item, incident on incident.
Sometimes the list comprises only single words, as in Murellus'
scolding of the plebeians in the opening scene. The listed details
convey both a strong sense of Rome's buildings and of the plebeians'
eagerness to welcome Caesar and to gain high vantage positions from
which to see the procession:

> Many a time and oft
> Have you climbed up to walls and battlements,
> To towers and windows, yea, to chimney tops
> *(Act 1 Scene 1, lines 36–8)*

Other lists build up detailed descriptions, as in Casca's record of earlier storms he has witnessed:

> I have seen tempests when the scolding winds
> Have rived the knotty oaks, and I have seen
> Th'ambitious ocean swell, and rage, and foam,
> To be exalted with the threatening clouds
>
> *(Act 1 Scene 3, lines 5–8)*

Similar descriptive lists include Calpurnia's account of 'most horrid sights seen by the watch':

> A lioness hath whelpèd in the streets,
> And graves have yawned and yielded up their dead;
> Fierce fiery warriors fight upon the clouds
> In ranks and squadrons and right form of war,
> Which drizzled blood upon the Capitol;
> The noise of battle hurtled in the air,
> Horses did neigh and dying men did groan,
> And ghosts did shriek and squeal about the streets.
>
> *(Act 2 Scene 2, lines 17–24)*

The effect of these descriptive lists is to expand the universe of the play. They operate as reminders that there are greater forces at work than those that can be controlled by the politicians of Rome. The significance of such natural and supernatural images and influences is discussed on pages 24–5.

In all lists in the play, an actor will seek to give each listed 'item' a distinctiveness in emphasis and emotional tone, and sometimes an accompanying action and expression. In addition, the cumulative effect of each list can add to the force of argument, enrich atmosphere, amplify meaning and provide extra dimensions of character. Both Brutus and Antony start their funeral orations with short lists to secure the attention of their listeners, and to establish a sense of shared identity: 'Romans, countrymen, and lovers . . .'; 'Friends, Romans, countrymen . . .'.

Verse and prose

How did Shakespeare decide whether to write in verse or prose? One answer is that he followed theatrical convention. Prose was traditionally used by comic and low-status characters. High-status characters spoke verse. Comic scenes were written in prose (as were letters), but audiences expected verse in serious scenes: the poetic style was thought to be particularly suitable for moments of high dramatic or emotional intensity, and for tragic themes.

With few exceptions, the verse of *Julius Caesar* is blank verse: unrhymed verse written in iambic pentameter. Iambic pentameter is a metre in which each line has five stressed syllables (/) alternating with five unstressed syllables (×):

> × / × / × / × / × /
> The angry spot doth glow on Caesar's brow

At school, Shakespeare had learned the technical definition of iambic pentameter. In Greek *penta* means 'five', and *iamb* means a 'foot' of two syllables, the first unstressed, the second stressed (as in the pronunciation of 'alas': aLAS). Shakespeare practised writing in that metre, and his early plays, such as *Titus Andronicus* or *Richard III*, tend to be very regular in rhythm (de-DUM de-DUM de-DUM de-DUM de-DUM), with each line 'end-stopped' (making sense on its own).

By the time he wrote *Julius Caesar* at the turn of the sixteenth century, Shakespeare was becoming more flexible and experimental in his use of iambic pentameter. The play's verse achieves greater maturity of feeling and expression than in earlier plays. The 'five-beat' metre is still often obvious, but at other times, notably in the night storm scene (Act 1 Scene 3), it is less prominent. End-stopped lines are less frequent. There is greater use of *enjambement* (running on) where one line flows on into the next, seemingly with little or no pause. Shakespeare plays sentences and clauses against lines of set length, as in Cassius' disdain for Casca's fear:

> You are dull, Casca, and those sparks of life
> That should be in a Roman you do want,
> Or else you use not. You look pale, and gaze,
> And put on fear, and cast yourself in wonder
> To see the strange impatience of the heavens.
>
> *(Act 1 Scene 3, lines 57–61)*

Critical approaches

Traditional criticism

Julius Caesar has been among the most frequently performed and popular of Shakespeare's plays. Shakespeare himself recalled it in *Hamlet*. When Hamlet asks Polonius about his acting experience at university, Polonius replies, 'I did enact Julius Caesar. I was killed i' th' Capitol. Brutus killed me.' Shakespeare appreciated, too, with what force the murder of Caesar had struck the minds of statesmen and scholars through the centuries before his time, and how its dramatic potential might resound through future years. So, in a striking premonition, he has Cassius say:

> How many ages hence
> Shall this our lofty scene be acted over
> In states unborn and accents yet unknown!
> *(Act 3 Scene 1, lines 111–13)*

As early as 1599 Thomas Platter judged a performance of the play excellent (see page 99), but it is generally agreed that serious criticism of *Julius Caesar* began in the eighteenth century with Doctor Samuel Johnson, who, with typical directness, found the play

> somewhat cold and unaffecting comparing with some other of Shakespeare's plays; his adherence to the real story, and to Roman manners, seems to have impeded the natural vigour of his genius.

Samuel Taylor Coleridge found a more specific difficulty in Shakespeare's selection of material. In 1808 he remained puzzled by Brutus and by Shakespeare's omission of Caesar's past actions:

> How too could Brutus say he finds no personal cause; i.e. none in Caesar's past conduct as a man? Had he not passed the Rubicon? Entered Rome as a conqueror? Placed his Gauls in the Senate? Shakespeare (it may be said) has not brought these things forward. True! And this is just the ground of my

perplexity. What character does Shakespeare mean his Brutus to be?

Writing nine years later, and swayed by his ardent sympathies with the ideals of the French Revolution, William Hazlitt, too, was prompted to comment on Brutus and on the contrast between Brutus and Cassius. The failure of the conspiracy, he felt, was due to 'the generous temper of Brutus':

> Cassius was better cut out for a conspirator. His heart prompted his head. His habitual jealousy made him fear the worst that might happen, and his irritability of temper added to his inveteracy of purpose, and sharpened his patriotism.

The comments of both Coleridge and Hazlitt have critical significance because they display one of the major features of traditional writing about the play: character criticism.

The critic with whom the expression 'character study' is most associated is A C Bradley. Around 100 years ago, Bradley delivered a course of lectures at Oxford University which were published in 1904 as *Shakespearean Tragedy*. The book has never been out of print, and Bradley's approach has been hugely influential. Although Bradley makes only passing references to *Julius Caesar* (he is centrally concerned with *Hamlet, Macbeth, Othello* and *King Lear*), his form of criticism reflects previous approaches to the play, and has strongly influenced critical approaches right up to the present day. In a typical passage Bradley traced a connection between character qualities found in Shakespeare's earlier plays to their development in later tragedies:

> Both Brutus and Hamlet are highly intellectual by nature and reflective by habit. Both may even be called, in a popular sense, philosophic; Brutus may be called so in a stricter sense. Each, being also a 'good' man, shows accordingly, when placed in critical circumstances, a sensitive and almost painful anxiety to do right.

Bradley talks of the characters in Shakespeare as if they were real human beings, existing in worlds recognisable to modern readers. He identifies the unique desires and motives which give characters their particular personalities, and which evoke feelings of admiration or disapproval in the audience. Assuming that each character experiences familiar human emotions and thoughts, Bradley's presentation of conflict in Shakespeare's tragedies is primarily that within the individual, an inward struggle. Bradley's reading of Aristotle shifted the meaning of *hamartia* (error of judgement) to 'tragic or fatal flaw'. Bradley sees each hero in Shakespeare's tragedies as struggling with circumstances and fate, and afflicted with a personal defect which causes the tragedy:

> a marked one-sidedness, a predisposition in some particular direction; a total incapacity, in certain circumstances, of resisting the force which draws in this direction; a fatal tendency to identify the whole being with one interest, object, passion or habit of mind. This, it would seem, is, for Shakespeare, the fundamental tragic trait . . . some marked imperfection or defect: irresolution, precipitancy, pride, credulousness, excessive simplicity, excessive susceptibility to sexual emotions and the like . . . these contribute decisively to the conflict and catastrophe.

Bradley's character approach has been much criticised. For example, it is evident that most of Shakespeare's tragic characters possess more than 'one interest, object, passion or habit of mind'. Both Caesar and Brutus – each of whom has a claim to tragic heroism – are motivated by more complex forces than Bradley's model seems to require. For instance, a number of factors seem to come together to bring about the collapse of Brutus' hopes: his obsession with honour, his naivety in believing that other people have the same steadfastness he has, his incautious generosity towards Antony, his sublimation of his grief over Portia's death by insisting on marching to Philippi. A second criticism is that a focus on character neglects the Elizabethan contexts of the play's creation: the cultural and intellectual assumptions of the time, stage conditions, and poetic and dramatic conventions. The Contexts section (see pages 64–79) demonstrates the powerful influence on *Julius Caesar* of such factors.

The most frequent objection to Bradley is his treatment of characters as real people. Modern criticism is uneasy about discussing characters in this way, preferring to see them as fictional creations in a stage drama. But although Bradley has fallen from critical favour, his influence is still evident. As page 121 shows, it is difficult to avoid talking or writing about characters as if they were living people and making moral judgements on them. Bradley's notion of a 'predisposition in some particular direction' has proved similarly powerful, for instance in the interpretation that sees Brutus as being too rigidly governed by his ideals.

Following Bradley, and accepting his assumptions, Caroline Spurgeon opened up a fresh perspective on *Julius Caesar*: the study of its imagery. In *Shakespeare's Imagery and What it Tells Us* (1935), Spurgeon identifies patterns of imagery in each of Shakespeare's plays. She finds *Julius Caesar* has 'relatively few images . . . they are clear, definite, and worked out in a full and leisurely way'. As an example of what she calls the 'slow' working out of images, she cites Antony's comparison of Lepidus to an ass turned out to graze:

> He shall but bear them as the ass bears gold,
> To groan and sweat under the business,
> Either led or driven, as we point the way;
> And having brought our treasure where we will,
> Then take we down his load and turn him off
> (Like to the empty ass) to shake his ears
> And graze in commons.   (*Act 4 Scene 1, lines 21–7*)

The value of Caroline Spurgeon's pioneering study of Shakespeare's imagery has been acknowledged by later critics, but her work has also been much criticised. She only occasionally examines how the imagery relates to the dramatic context of the play. Further, Spurgeon's claim that *Julius Caesar* 'has relatively few images' suggests that she worked with a somewhat restricted notion of imagery. The opening scene alone is rich in imagery. Murellus calls the common people 'You blocks, you stones'. When they saw Pompey's chariot, they cheered, 'That Tiber trembled underneath her banks'. Now they cheer Caesar, who 'comes in triumph over Pompey's blood'. Flavius tells them to weep their tears into the Tiber 'till the lowest stream / Do kiss the most exalted shores of all.' The decorations to be removed from Caesar's statues are 'These growing feathers plucked from Caesar's wing'.

Other critics followed Spurgeon's example in paying detailed attention to the language and images of the play. G Wilson Knight's *The Imperial Theme* (1931) contains two important essays on the play. In the first, 'The Torch of Life', he draws together patterns which are developed through certain key images and concepts: metallic imagery, love, blood, weeping, the body, fire and spirit. Wilson Knight concludes from the recurrence of these thematic elements that the central action in the play is the severance of 'spirit' from 'matter':

> In Shakespeare 'creation' is the result of blending elements, the
> divine and the earthly. These are mated. Here they are
> unmated. And chaos, past, present, future are all jumbled
> together . . . Neither spirit nor matter are now real, the fusion
> on which each depends is gone. Matter uninfused with spirit is
> illogical: spirit naked is terrible.

Wilson Knight's argument is that Caesar existed as body and spirit. The physical matter that was Caesar's body was subject to the increasing weakness of age. It was not his body that made him extraordinary, but his spirit. The killing of Caesar does not destroy his spirit, as Brutus hoped, but in severing spirit from matter, the process of creation is reversed and Rome is plunged into chaos. In a second essay, 'The Eroticism of *Julius Caesar*', Wilson Knight distinguishes Brutus from Antony and Cassius, in that Brutus has a divided view of Caesar and places honour before love.

Stimulating and exciting though Wilson Knight's interpretations remain for many readers, his exuberant, often declamatory style, and his metaphysical interpretations are considered by more recent critics to be no longer academically appropriate. His sense that after Brutus' death 'Rome is crowned again with peace' and that 'the wound heals, Antony's love for Caesar avenges his death, peace is restored' has been overtaken by a far more realistic, if not cynical, view of Antony as a political opportunist and of Octavius as a cold, efficient, ruthlessly calculating young man whose time is yet to come. Yet Wilson Knight's concentration on identifying themes and arguing that the play projects certain values has given his work an enduring relevance.

While Spurgeon and Wilson Knight had moved beyond considering character as pre-eminent in discussing Shakespeare's plays, Bradley's work on the four great tragedies has remained influential. J I M Stewart's *Character and Motive in Shakespeare* (1949) finds Brutus' motives confused, if not dishonest:

> How came Brutus to join the conspirators? There is an element of unresolved mystery here . . . It is clear that he is concerned for his own disinterestedness. He fumbles after some interpretation of the situation whereby it shall appear to be the whole body of the people who are endangered by tyranny. Yet his final adherence to the plot is insufficiently considered and a matter of obscure emotions at play behind the stoic mask.

Stewart follows the Bradley approach in displaying a concentration on character, and, in the Bradley tradition, finds Caesar's 'But I am constant as the northern star' to be evidence of Caesar's own awareness of the personality cult (Caesarism) he has created. Caesar's words resound with a certainty of his own indestructibility, but Stewart comments: 'It is something which cannot but escape the daggers of the conspirators, for it is an idea and mocks their thrusts.'

Anne Righter, in *Shakespeare and the Idea of the Play* (1962), provides yet another focus for criticism in finding a distinctively Shakespearean consciousness of theatricality in *Julius Caesar*. Selecting Casca's report of Caesar's rejecting the proffered crown before the assembled plebeians, who 'clap him and hiss him according as he pleased and displeased them, as they use to do the players in the theatre' (Act 1 Scene 2, lines 252–4), she identifies this theatrical image as a reminder of the precarious position of any ruler, 'a fatal division between individual and crown'. Righter also discusses Brutus' later exhortation to the conspirators:

> Let not our looks put on our purposes,
> But bear it as our Roman actors do,
> With untired spirits and formal constancy.
>
> *(Act 2 Scene 1, lines 225–7)*

She sees Brutus here making an appeal for reality 'to draw its strength from illusion, reversing the usual order'. In this and in the exultant cries of Cassius and Brutus as they contemplate the future re-enactment of the murder of Caesar ('this our lofty scene') she finds textual evidence of a particular function of the Elizabethan stage:

The actors, Shakespeare's own companions and friends, have become the chroniclers of man's great deeds. It is in the theatre that the noble actions of the world are preserved for the instruction of future generations.

Reinforcing the shift away from a concentration solely on character analysis, L C Knights attempts to link character with its social context, and explores the relationship between personal and public life as it emerges in the play. For Knights, the question that Shakespeare poses is 'What happens when personal judgement tries to move exclusively on a political plane, where issues are simplified and distorted?' The play's balance of domestic and private life, marriage and close friendship, 'where truth between man and man resides' against the words and actions of the public arena is the dramatic context within which Brutus is central: 'It is this Brutus, the close friend of Caesar, who wrenches his mind to divorce policy from friendship.' In seeing in the play 'Shakespeare's developing preoccupation with the relation between political action and morality', Knights is a forerunner of critical debate concerned with political aspects of the plays.

Two examples of critical response which have opened up the plays to less traditional lines of enquiry and which can usefully prepare for a discussion of more recent critical approaches are Robert Miola's *Shakespeare's Rome* (1983) and Sigurd Burckhardt's *Shakespearean Meanings* (1968). For Miola, place is important:

> Sharply defined by recognisable localities such as the Capitol, marketplace, and walls, Rome is the central protagonist in the play. The city again shapes the lives of its inhabitants, who struggle to act according to Roman heroic traditions . . . The ideals of honour and constancy here make up the moral universe.

Burckhardt discerns an intriguing time pattern in the play (see page 71). He observes the uncertainty associated with time in Act 2 Scene 1, and then notes that Caesar's institution of the Julian calendar and Pope Gregory's reform of the Julian calendar in 1582 both provoked a degree of social disaffection:

Thus at the turn of the century – Shakespeare wrote *Julius Caesar* in 1599 – a situation existed in Europe exactly analogous to that of Rome in 44 BC. It was a time of confusion and uncertainty, when the most basic category by which men order their experience seemed to have become unstable and untrustworthy, subject to arbitrary political manipulation.

Burckhardt's persuasive thesis relating the anxieties of Caesar's Rome with those of late sixteenth-century Europe gives his approach a refreshing historical basis.

Modern criticism

Modern criticism argues that traditional approaches to *Julius Caesar*, with their focus on character, are somewhat reductive. The concentration on personal response ignores society and history, and so divorces literary, dramatic and aesthetic matters from their social context. Contemporary critical perspectives therefore shift the focus from individuals to how the social conditions of Republican Rome (and Elizabethan England) are reflected in characters' relationships, language and behaviour. Modern criticism also concerns itself with how changing social assumptions at different periods of time have affected interpretations of the play.

Political criticism

'Political criticism' is a convenient label for approaches concerned with power and social structure. Such approaches to *Julius Caesar* are less concerned with traditional discussions of character or with the focus on Brutus as the centre of the tragedy, than with historical realities of political, economic and military power, both in Shakespeare's time and our own.

Richard Wilson's approach to the play is to relate the ideas of authority and power in *Julius Caesar* to the imposition of control over theatrical excesses in London in the closing years of the sixteenth century. Wilson sees the tribunes' disapproval of the plebeians who were celebrating the arrival of Caesar in the opening scene as reflecting the authority which, by 1612, had abolished 'all Jigs, Rhymes and Dances after Plays' to prevent 'tumults and outrages whereby His Majesty's peace is often broke'. The theatres were recognised as being a potential threat to the stable order of the state, but Wilson argues that a possible interpretation of the opening line ('Hence! Home, you idle creatures, get you home!') could be that Shakespeare's company was declaring that their theatre was legitimate and no place for 'idle' workers:

> The first words uttered on the stage of the Globe can be interpreted, then, as a manoeuvre in the campaign to legitimise the Shakespearean stage and dissociate it from the subversiveness of London's artisanal subculture.

Throughout the 1590s there were eruptions of public disorder in London as workers rioted. Theatres which staged popular attractions drew London's disaffected workers (London's equivalent of the Roman plebeians) and so were venues of likely public disturbances. Wilson argues that one of the responses to these outbreaks was to attempt to control 'the language of carnival', to ensure that theatrical performance was subject to licensing:

> This premiere Globe play reflects candidly on the process whereby hegemony is obtained through the control of discourse . . . Victory in *Julius Caesar* goes to those who administer and distribute the access to discourse, and the conspirators lose possession of the initiative in the action from the instant they concede Antony to 'speak in the order of [the] funeral'.

In making issues of social control central, especially through the control of discourse, Wilson's approach examines the historical parallels between Caesar's Rome and Shakespeare's London, as well as the contemporary political conflicts which Shakespeare used the theatre to articulate. He identifies how actions must be understood not only in the context of the social world of the play, but also as reflecting the social and economic structures within which Shakespeare was working.

Many productions in the second half of the twentieth century attempted to find political significance in the play through indicating its parallels with modern political developments. For more extended discussion of these, see pages 101–4.

Feminist criticism

Feminism aims to achieve rights and equality for women in social, political and economic life. It challenges sexism: those beliefs and practices which result in the degradation, oppression and subordination of women. Feminist critics therefore reject 'male ownership' of criticism, in which men determined what questions were to be asked of a play, and which answers were acceptable. They argue that male criticism often neglects, represses or misrepresents female experience, and stereotypes or distorts women's points of view.

Feminist criticism, like any 'approach', takes a wide variety of forms. Nonetheless, it is possible to identify certain major concerns for feminist critical writing on *Julius Caesar*. Most commonly, feminists approach the play using the notion of patriarchy (male domination of women). Feminists point to the fact that throughout much of history, power has been in the hands of men, both in society and in the family. In the subordinate roles of Calpurnia and Portia, *Julius Caesar* clearly reflects that patriarchal control, and feminists see the issue of unjust male power and control as crucial to understanding Rome.

The work of Mary Hamer provides a convenient example of a feminist approach to the play. She draws attention to Brutus' treatment of Portia in Act 2 Scene 1:

> To a woman's ear, the ear of a woman who has been married more than once, as I have, and as indeed the historical Portia herself had been, the words of Brutus strike a familiar note. The wife takes her husband by surprise; 'What are you doing here?' he asks, rather put out as the broken movement of his first line shows: 'Portia! What mean you? Wherefore rise you now?' (Act 2 Scene 1, line 234). As a form of greeting this leaves something to be desired, the more so, perhaps if we hear in it a muted and domestic echo of the tribunes' cry that opened the play: 'Hence! Home, you idle creatures, get you home!'

Hamer sees the wound that Portia gives herself as evidence that Portia has, in her 'good Roman education', learned the lessons designed for men: 'When it comes to bodies, there has been an attempt to educate both Brutus and Portia out of tenderness and respect.' On the other hand, the vividness of Calpurnia's description of her dream suggests that 'she has never had her mind trained to think like a man'. Hamer implies that Caesar's contempt for Calpurnia's dream is 'because the dream is produced not out of a book but out of her own woman's body, like her voice . . . It is because Caesar only pays attention to the voices of other men that he will defy Calpurnia's common sense and venture outside.'

Performance criticism

Performance criticism fully acknowledges that *Julius Caesar* is a play: a script to be performed by actors to an audience. It examines all aspects of the play in performance: its staging in the theatre or on film and video. Performance criticism focuses on Shakespeare's stagecraft and the semiotics of theatre (words, costumes, gestures, etc.) together with the 'afterlife' of the play (what happened to *Julius Caesar* after Shakespeare wrote it). That involves scrutiny of how productions at different periods have presented the play. As such, performance criticism appraises how the text has been cut, added to, rewritten and rearranged to present a version considered appropriate to the times.

Julius Caesar seems to have been a popular play right from the time it was first performed. Thomas Platter, who visited London from Switzerland in 1599, recorded:

> After lunch on September 21, at about two o'clock, I and my party crossed the river, and there in the house with the thatched roof we saw an excellent performance of the tragedy of the first Emperor Julius Caesar with about fifteen characters; after the play, according to their custom they did a most elegant and curious dance, two dressed in men's clothes, and two in women's.

There is little doubt that this was a performance of Shakespeare's *Julius Caesar*, one of the first plays to be performed by Shakespeare's own company at the newly built Globe Theatre.

What evidence exists suggests that as the seventeenth century reached its last decades, stagings tended to be based on severely modified and cut scripts. In the 1680s the actor–manager Thomas Betterton set a trend by playing Brutus as the central tragic hero of the play. Colley Cibber, a noted Shakespearean critic of the time, observed the restraint with which Betterton's Brutus was played:

When the Betterton Brutus was provoked in his dispute with
Cassius, his Spirit flew only to his Eye; his steady Look alone
supplied that Terror which he disdained an intemperance in
his Voice . . . Thus, with a settled Dignity of Contempt, like an
unheeding Rock he repelled upon himself the Foam of Cassius.

Eighteenth-century productions strove for a clarity that eliminated
the worrying complexities in Shakespeare's character portrayals. In an
'age of reason', it was not surprising that the intervention of the
supernatural was reduced to a minimum. In the Dryden–Davenant
version of the script, Brutus was made more clearly heroic, and was
given a more impressive death scene, in which he killed himself
unaided after delivering a powerfully patriotic death speech. The
central dramatic position given to Brutus dominated productions right
through the nineteenth century.

Staging priorities changed in the nineteenth century. Extravagant
stage scenery was used to present Rome in splendour. While the
actor–managers of the day endeavoured to reproduce authenticity of
architectural detail, they were not always meticulous over historical
accuracy. They tended to present features which reflected the
grandeur of imperial Rome rather than the relative austerity of the
Republic (as Rome still was at the end of Caesar's rule). John Philip
Kemble's 1812 production was noted for its impressive visual effects,
lavish scenery and costume, colourful, stately processions, carefully
grouped performers. There was a striving for aesthetic principles
articulated by Sir Joshua Reynolds' *Discourses on Art*. The priorities
were 'perfect form', 'ideal beauty' and 'nobleness of conception'.

With such emphasis on the visual effects on the stage, the text was
streamlined to afford a 'straight-line' production, again with Brutus
dying as a noble and idealised patriot, applauding his 'beloved
country'. Antony was played as a young, athletic nobleman driven only
by the purest of motives. Any suggestion of political opportunism was
excised from the text and the scene in which Antony, Lepidus and
Octavius draw up a death list of those Romans who had held positions
of influence and who might not support the new order of the
Triumvirate (Act 4 Scene 1) disappeared completely. This left Antony
as little more than Caesar's youthful friend and avenger. In the 1820s
William Charles Macready integrated the large number of actors who
were now required to represent the Roman plebeians more decisively

in the action. Formerly passive onlookers, they became a vigorous participating dramatic force, most notably in Macready's staging of the forum scene.

As the nineteenth century neared its close, the central dramatic position of Brutus was emphasised less. Herbert Beerbohm Tree's 1898 production emphasised the active involvement of the Roman crowds, and set out to make the forum scene the most prominent, with Antony as the leading role in the play. Convinced that his audiences wanted spectacle on a massive scale, Tree included a prelude of scenes depicting the daily life of Rome before the tribunes enter at the beginning of the play. Tree established three important new trends in his production. First, he released Antony from the traditional constraints that had limited his character portrayal, making him work hard to win the crowd's support. Second, by generating in the listeners at the funeral orations much more vociferousness and volatility in their reactions, Tree made the crowd scenes more dramatically decisive. Third, he chose for the role of Caesar an actor who gave to the character an individuality and a human complexity.

Across the Atlantic, the popularity of *Julius Caesar* during the nineteenth century took root for reasons associated with the political development of the United States. Revolutionary ideals struck a more immediate historical resonance in America than they did in England, and political oratory was closer to people's civic experience. Edwin Booth's New York production (1871) stands out as significant in developing Brutus' psychological complexity. He became more of a Romantic, his discernment and idealism arousing in him an aversion to violence which manifested itself in a deep reluctance to stab Caesar.

In Britain, the twentieth century saw a return to much simpler stagings of the play. Although the tradition of extravagant productions lingered on, most no longer attempted to create an impression of realism. Under the influence of William Poel and Harley Granville-Barker the stage was cleared of the clutter of historical detail. The aim was to recapture the conditions of the Elizabethan bare stage, which was not dependent on theatrical illusion. That implied a minimum of scenery, scenes flowing swiftly into each other, and a concern for the clear speaking of Shakespeare's language.

A new emphasis was given to aspects of the play by Orson Welles, whose 1937 production in the USA (subtitled 'Death of a Dictator') set a trend for staging the play as a comment on modern political developments of the time. The production used a severely cut text with an almost complete concentration on Caesar, Brutus, and the mob. Welles strove to use the play to make theatrical his sense of 'political violence and the moral duty of the individual in the face of tyranny'. Eighteen years later, the Mankiewicz–Houseman film of *Julius Caesar* incorporated a subtext which pointed to the rise and fall of Mussolini and Hitler. One reviewer of the film saw in the fate of Cinna the poet, a suggestion of 'the feverish witchhunt hysteria of the McCarthy red scare era'.

Through the 1960s and 1970s the exploration of modern contemporary events became a main motivation for staging the play. Trevor Nunn's 1972 production sought to make *Julius Caesar* a part of his Roman cycle of Shakespeare's four Roman plays (*Titus Andronicus, Coriolanus, Julius Caesar* and *Antony and Cleopatra*) which aimed to chart the rise and fall of the Roman state through 'tribalism, authoritarianism, to colonialism, to decadence'. One significant outcome was the conspicuousness of Octavius' dramatic importance in *Julius Caesar*, foreshadowing his role in *Antony and Cleopatra*.

Other productions with strong modern contemporary references include one in Stratford, Connecticut (1979) with Caesar as a Latin American dictator, and the crowd as tourists all brandishing cameras. In Belfast (1981) a production drew a parallel with the assassination of Egypt's President Sadat. An Oregon Festival production prompted one reviewer to identify Caesar with Che Guevara. Stage productions have also mirrored political developments in Eastern Europe. A Royal Shakespeare Company production in 1993 gave the play a contemporary post-cold-war resonance, paralleling the assassination of Caesar with the toppling of East European dictators. A 2001 RSC production reflected Germany of the 1930s and 1940s. The first scene was cut from the production and the senators entered with a song celebrating the power of Rome.

The 1970s saw some attempts to dispense with the crowds on the stage, but most critics agreed that the experiment failed, robbing the forum scene of its necessary tension. Particularly in the closing decades of the twentieth century, and in the twenty-first, productions have remained alert to modern political relevance and to probing the play for underlying questions about the extent to which human beings are manipulators or victims of the forces which shape political destiny.

One of the most impressive stagings of *Julius Caesar* was Peter Stein's 1992 Salzburg Festival production. Using a vast open-air stage 45 metres wide, with a sliding roof and a colonnaded back wall hewn from solid rock, Stein was able to employ a cast of 37, complemented by 200 local amateurs and students. One reviewer commented:

> This gave the crowd scenes a seething vitality . . . The Feast of Lupercal becomes a huge purification ritual with body-painted shepherd figures hurtling through the mob and the boxer-like Mark Antony pummelling Calpurnia for luck . . . In the forum scene Brutus and Mark Antony are confronted not by the usual apologetic handful but by a milling, angry, boiler-suited crowd.

After the killing of Caesar, the assassins simply stood gazing silently at his corpse in awed astonishment at what they had done. The murder was not staged as a 'big production number, but a numbing, desperate, terrifying act carried out in broad daylight'. The theatre critic Michael Billington found the production a compelling evocation of the play:

> What he has done is to reach to its political heart. By combining togas and suits . . . he has managed to evoke ancient and modern worlds. By switching between day and night, bringing the covered roof to evoke the cometary exhalations of the storm scene, he has caught exactly the sense of a city in turmoil.

In 1993 the RSC staged a 'promenade' production in its smallest theatre, The Other Place. The actors moved among the audience, who became the citizens of Rome. The play was placed in a modern setting with Caesar as a silver-haired figure whom some took to be Boris Yeltsin, though most reviewers identified it as Ceausescu (Communist dictator of Romania, and one of the several Eastern European rulers deposed after the fall of the Berlin Wall in 1990). The uncertainty was provocative, for Yeltsin was, at the time, favourably regarded by the West, whereas Ceausescu was not. Caesar was followed by a TV camera and a secret policeman. The final battles, with their images of rape and bereaved mothers, inevitably recalled the tragedy of Bosnia.

The parallel with modern contemporary politics was made clear in the programme, which printed a calendar of political events from 1985, and the action was accordingly transplanted to a vaguely Eastern European dictatorship. The banners, whose crests were slashed out when Caesar was assassinated, recalled the similarly gaping flags during the revolution in Romania. A difficulty with giving the play a specific modern political relevance is that contemporary audiences are likely to be insufficiently distanced from issues emerging in the play. The balance which Shakespeare has written into the play is easily lost. As one reviewer put it, 'it is hardly respectful to the crowds that outfaced Ceausescu or were mown down in Tiananmen Square, to compare them to the throng in *Julius Caesar*, which has no firm principles and simply responds to skilful demagoguery'. Another reviewer had similar reservations:

> If you identify this with Ceausescu land, what are you to make of Shakespeare's debate about the morality of assassination, or, indeed, of Brutus' own ethical conflict about killing a revered idol . . . Whatever the tempting parallels, you cannot escape the fact that this is a play about Imperial Rome.

In May 1999, the newly constructed Globe Theatre on London's Bankside staged a 500th anniversary production of *Julius Caesar*. It was remarkable not for any special interpretative slant, but for its historical reconstruction. Even a 'final company jig' was added at the end, recalling Platter's 1599 record of 'a most elegant and curious dance'. Most of the actors wore sumptuous Elizabethan dress, with the principal characters donning togas and helmets at times. The Globe audience were addressed as the Roman crowd, though dotted among them were actors – plebeians and the Soothsayer – wearing T-shirts and baseball caps. The sense of three time levels was effective because, in one reviewer's words, '*Julius Caesar* is simultaneously a play about the Romans, the Elizabethans and . . . the way we live now. When Cinna the poet is brutally killed by the mob, we might be watching today's football thugs.'

Psychoanalytic criticism
In the twentieth century, psychoanalysis became a major influence on the understanding and interpretation of human behaviour. The

founder of psychoanalysis, Sigmund Freud, explained personality as the result of unconscious and irrational desires, repressed memories or wishes, sexuality, fantasy, anxiety and conflict. Freud's theories have had a strong influence on criticism and stagings of Shakespeare's plays, most obviously on *Hamlet*, in the well-known claim that Hamlet suffers from an Oedipus complex.

Julius Caesar has attracted comparatively little psychoanalytic critical writing. As Norman Holland points out, such critics usually discuss the play in relation to their analysis of *Hamlet*. Holland's book, *Psychoanalysis and Shakespeare*, details the major features of psychoanalytic interpretations of *Julius Caesar*:

- Brutus, like Hamlet, has murderous impulses towards a fatherlike man.
- Because Brutus has no mother to inhibit his murderous desires, he acts them out, assassinating Caesar.
- The other conspirators also represent a 'decomposed' or fragmented Oedipal son.
- Cassius embodies the self-punishing side of Brutus, obsessed with suicide.
- Antony embodies the filial piety of Brutus, his love for Caesar.
- Caesar's ghost signifies the persistence of Brutus' infantile feelings towards his 'father' (Caesar).
- Brutus' statement that he loves 'Rome more' symbolises a mother figure, and so can provide an Oedipal reading of the play.
- Brutus is motivated by unconscious envy of Caesar, but uses reason to cover his resentment. The basis for his envy is self-love.
- Brutus fails because he unconsciously wishes to punish himself for killing Caesar.
- Brutus is the victim of his own tyrannical superego, which drives him to consider himself superior to others.

Such interpretations fail to give a coherent view of the whole play, tending to view it as an Oedipal fantasy (Brutus' desire to kill his 'father', Caesar). They reveal the obvious weaknesses in applying psychoanalytic theories to *Julius Caesar*. They cannot be proved or disproved, they neglect historical, political and social factors which are fundamental to the play, and they are highly speculative. Psychoanalytic approaches are therefore often accused of imposing interpretations based on theory rather than on Shakespeare's text. Nonetheless, the play has obvious features which seem to invite psychoanalytic approaches, including Calpurnia's dream and Caesar's ghost.

Postmodern criticism

Postmodern criticism (sometimes called 'deconstruction') is not always easy to understand because it is not centrally concerned with consistency or reasoned argument. It does not accept that one section of the story is necessarily connected to what follows, or that characters relate to each other in meaningful ways. Because of such assumptions, postmodern criticism is sometimes described as 'reading against the grain' or less politely as 'textual harassment'. The approach therefore has obvious drawbacks in providing a model for examination students who are expected to display reasoned, coherent argument, and respect for the evidence of the text.

Postmodernism often revels in the cleverness of its own use of language, and accepts all kinds of anomalies and contradictions in a spirit of playfulness or 'carnival'. It abandons any notion of the organic unity of the play, and rejects the assumption that a Shakespeare play possesses clear patterns or themes. Some postmodern critics even deny the possibility of finding meaning in language. They claim that words simply refer to other words, and so any interpretation is endlessly delayed (or 'deferred', as the deconstructionists say).

Postmodern approaches to *Julius Caesar* are most clearly seen in stage productions. There, you could think of it as simply 'a mixture of styles'. The label 'postmodern' is applied to productions which self-consciously show little regard for consistency in character, or for coherence in telling the story. Characters are dressed in costumes from very different historical periods, and carry both modern and ancient weapons. Ironically, Shakespeare himself has been regarded as a postmodern writer for the way he mixes genres in his plays, combining comedy with tragedy.

Organising your responses

The purpose of this section is to help you improve your writing about *Julius Caesar*. It offers practical guidance on two kinds of tasks: writing about an extract from the play and writing an essay.

Writing about an extract

It is an expected part of all Shakespeare study that you should be able to write well about an extract (sometimes called a 'passage') from the play. An extract is usually between 30 and 70 lines long, and you are invited to comment on it. The instructions vary. Sometimes the task is very briefly expressed:

- Write a detailed commentary on the following passage.
  or
- Write about the effect of the extract on your own thoughts and feelings.

At other times a particular focus is specified for your writing:

- With close reference to the language and imagery of the passage, show in what ways it helps to establish important issues in the play.
  or
- Analyse the style and structure of the extract, showing what it contributes to your appreciation of the play's major concerns.

In writing your response, you must of course take account of the precise wording of the task, and ensure you concentrate on each particular point specified. But however the invitation to write about an extract is expressed, it requires you to comment in detail on the language. You should identify and evaluate how the language reveals character, creates context, contributes to plot development, offers opportunities for dramatic effect, and embodies crucial concerns for the play as a whole. These 'crucial concerns' are also referred to as 'themes' or 'issues' or 'preoccupations' of the play.

The following framework is a guide to how you can write a detailed commentary on an extract. Writing a paragraph on each item will help you bring out the meaning and significance of the extract, and show how Shakespeare achieves his effects.

Paragraph 1: Locate the extract in the play and say who is on stage.
Paragraph 2: State what the extract is about and identify its structure.
Paragraph 3: Identify the mood or atmosphere of the extract.

Paragraphs 4–8:	These paragraphs analyse how
Diction (vocabulary)	Shakespeare achieves his effects. They
Imagery	concentrate on the language of the
Antithesis	extract, showing the dramatic effect of
Repetition	each item, and how the language
Lists	expresses crucial concerns of the play.

Paragraph 9: Staging opportunities
Paragraph 10: Conclusion

The following example uses the framework to show how the paragraphs making up the essay might be written. The extract includes Brutus' soliloquy about the necessity of Caesar's death. The framework headings (in bold), would not, of course, appear in your essay. They are presented only to help you to see how the framework is used.

Extract

Brutus' orchard Night
Enter BRUTUS

BRUTUS   What, Lucius, ho!
    I cannot by the progress of the stars
    Give guess how near to day. Lucius, I say!
    I would it were my fault to sleep so soundly.
    When, Lucius, when? Awake, I say! What, Lucius!   5

Enter LUCIUS

LUCIUS   Called you, my lord?
BRUTUS   Get me a taper in my study, Lucius.
    When it is lighted, come and call me here.
LUCIUS   I will, my lord.   *Exit*
BRUTUS   It must be by his death. And for my part   10

I know no personal cause to spurn at him
But for the general. He would be crowned:
How that might change his nature, there's the question.
It is the bright day that brings forth the adder
And that craves wary walking. Crown him that, 15
And then I grant we put a sting in him
That at his will he may do danger with.
Th'abuse of greatness is when it disjoins
Remorse from power. And to speak truth of Caesar,
I have not known when his affections swayed 20
More than his reason. But 'tis a common proof
That lowliness is young ambition's ladder,
Whereto the climber-upward turns his face;
But when he once attains the upmost round
He then unto the ladder turns his back, 25
Looks in the clouds, scorning the base degrees
By which he did ascend. So Caesar may.
Then lest he may, prevent. And since the quarrel
Will bear no colour for the thing he is,
Fashion it thus: that what he is, augmented, 30
Would run to these and these extremities.
And therefore think him as a serpent's egg
(Which, hatched, would as his kind grow mischievous)
And kill him in the shell.

Enter LUCIUS

LUCIUS   The taper burneth in your closet, sir. 35
          Searching the window for a flint, I found
          This paper, thus sealed up, and I am sure
          It did not lie there when I went to bed.
Gives him the letter
BRUTUS   Get you to bed again, it is not day.
          Is not tomorrow, boy, the Ides of March? 40
LUCIUS   I know not, sir.
BRUTUS   Look in the calendar and bring me word.
LUCIUS   I will, sir.   *Exit*
BRUTUS   The exhalations whizzing in the air
          Give so much light that I may read by them. 45

Opens the letter and reads

    'Brutus, thou sleep'st. Awake, and see thyself!
    Shall Rome, etc. Speak, strike, redress!'
    'Brutus, thou sleep'st. Awake!'
    Such instigations have been often dropped
    Where I have took them up.   50
    'Shall Rome, etc.' Thus must I piece it out:
    Shall Rome stand under one man's awe? What, Rome?
    My ancestors did from the streets of Rome
    The Tarquin drive when he was called a king.
    'Speak, strike, redress!' Am I entreated   55
    To speak and strike? O Rome, I make thee promise,
    If the redress will follow, thou receivest
    Thy full petition at the hand of Brutus.

Enter LUCIUS

LUCIUS   Sir, March is wasted fifteen days.
Knock within
BRUTUS   'Tis good. Go to the gate, somebody knocks.   60

                                            [*Exit* LUCIUS]

    Since Cassius first did whet me against Caesar
    I have not slept.
    Between the acting of a dreadful thing
    And the first motion, all the interim is
    Like a phantasma or a hideous dream.   65
    The genius and the mortal instruments
    Are then in council, and the state of a man,
    Like to a little kingdom, suffers then
    The nature of an insurrection.   *(Act 2 Scene 1, lines 1–69)*

Paragraph 1: Locate the extract in the play and say who is onstage.
The extract is dramatically pivotal, for it reveals the conflict within
Brutus as he comes to the conclusion that Caesar must die. The scene
is set in Brutus' orchard. It is late at night after Brutus has listened
to Cassius' persuasive arguments about Caesar's tyrannical wielding
of power. Brutus has promised to give Cassius' argument further
thought, and in his soliloquy he does so. Brutus is onstage
throughout. Lucius makes three brief appearances.

Paragraph 2: State what the extract is about and identify its structure.
(Begin with one or two sentences identifying what the extract is about, followed by several sentences briefly identifying its structure, that is, the different sections of the extract.)

Brutus is unable to sleep because of the conflict in his mind about the danger of Caesar's excessive use of power. He concludes that Caesar must be killed to prevent Rome falling under totalitarian power, but he remains unhappy with the conclusion he has reached. Lucius, his young servant, brings him a letter (actually written by Cassius) which Brutus believes is a genuine reminder that he has a duty to defend Rome against the threat of Caesar's tyranny.

The extract falls into two major sections: the dialogues between Brutus and Lucius and the soliloquies of Brutus. Lucius is woken at the start of the scene, and is sent to light a candle in Brutus' study, leaving Brutus alone. Lucius returns, bringing the letter, and is sent off again to check the date, once more leaving Brutus alone onstage. Again, Lucius returns, and is sent to answer the knocking at the gate, leaving Brutus to reflect on his feelings.

Paragraph 3: Identify the mood or atmosphere of the extract.
There is a dark, brooding restlessness in the scene, as Brutus wrestles with the dilemma in his mind. He contemplates assassination as the only way to halt Caesar's growing power over Rome, yet he cannot commit himself to the act. The darkness seems to pervade the atmosphere, and despite the fact that Lucius has lit the candle in the study, Brutus remains under the night sky, where he reads the letter by starlight. There is a sense of a 'lull before the storm', which is broken by the arrival of the conspirators.

Paragraph 4: Diction
The language of Brutus, of Lucius and of the letter which Brutus reads is direct and uncomplicated. But below the surface of the words themselves there is a complex psychological movement. Brutus' 'Fashion it thus' is significant in revealing that his character is more susceptible to deviousness than he would like to acknowledge. He seems to be in the process of denying his own decent instincts; he has to shape his conclusion in a way that is convenient rather than honest. As he describes it, the process of climbing the ladder of ambition seems to become easier as the top is reached: 'climber-upward'

suggests the strain of the climb, 'attains' reflects the sense of achievement, and 'did ascend' implies a lack of self-exertion. The underlying suggestion seems to be that once at the top of the ladder one feels godlike. Brutus tends, also, to use unspecific terms in imagining Caesar's danger: 'what he is, augmented, / Would run to these and these extremities'. And later he makes an unspecified promise to Rome, speaking of 'the redress' and 'Thy full petition' without elaborating. The imperatives in the letter are strong, forceful words: 'Awake!', 'Speak, strike, redress!', which urge action without pause for thought. In the closing lines of the extract, Brutus refers to 'the acting of a dreadful thing'. The word 'whet' (line 61) has a powerful resonance. Its meaning (to sharpen) foreshadows the cutting edges of the knives that will stab Caesar. The letter's urging Brutus to 'Awake, and see thyself!' is ironic, coming after Brutus has woken Lucius, wishing 'it were my fault to sleep so soundly'. The line 'Brutus, thou sleep'st', seems to accuse Brutus of being oblivious of the danger Caesar poses to democratic Rome.

Paragraph 5: Imagery

Three key images give striking imaginative and intellectual force to the extract: the adder/serpent, the ladder and man as a kingdom. Brutus sees the growing power of Caesar as 'the bright day that brings forth the adder / And that craves wary walking'. The image is memorable because of the powerful contrast of the skyward openness of 'bright day' and the furtive ground movement of the 'adder'. A further implication is that the consequences of complacency will affect everyone's ordinary everyday actions ('walking'). Brutus sees the intoxication of success for those with ambition as a ladder, essential for early success, to which the climber 'turns his back' as he 'Looks in the clouds'. The different words used for gaining height (see diction, above) reinforce the change of the climber's attitude from initial humility to later contempt for what was once essential to him. Caesar, with all the unpredictability of the ambitious man, is best treated 'as a serpent's egg / (Which, hatched, would as his kind grow mischievous)'. That he should be killed 'in the shell' reveals both the advantage which the conspirators will have over Caesar, and his unsuspecting vulnerability. Brutus' view of man is as a microcosm of the state. The 'genius' sitting locked in 'council' with 'the mortal instruments' suggests that one's guiding spirit (mind) is in debate with one's physical being (body), just as debate takes place in a council chamber. Both the individual and the state are political, and so subject to division. So 'the state of a man' is like 'a little kingdom', normally orderly, but at crucial moments overwhelmed by the forces of 'an insurrection'.

Paragraph 6: Antithesis

In order to reveal the troubled state of Brutus' mind, Shakespeare has given him a series of antitheses, setting word against word in sharp opposition. Brutus' mental conflict emerges in a range of oppositions. 'Personal' is set against 'general', 'bright day' against 'adder', 'Crown' against 'sting', 'Remorse' against 'power', 'affections' (meaning emotions) against 'reason', 'lowliness' against 'ambition', 'face' against 'back', 'clouds' against 'base degrees', 'may' (suggesting permitted possibility) against 'prevent', 'is' against 'Would run', 'hatched' against 'kill', 'sleep'st' against 'Awake!', 'dropped' against 'took . . . up', 'Speak' against 'strike'. The extreme range of these polarised antitheses reveals the truth of Brutus' earlier admission to Cassius: 'poor Brutus [is] with himself at war'.

Paragraph 7: Repetition

Different kinds of repetition pervade the language of the extract, each serving varied dramatic purposes. Brutus repeats the name 'Lucius' four times in his opening five lines. This is partly to establish the dramatic situation, with a restless Brutus having to rouse a sleeping servant, and also to lodge in the minds of the audience the name of Lucius (the bearer of light). Lucius' repeated use of 'my lord' and 'sir' indicates his respect for, and willingness to please, Brutus.

In the soliloquy (lines 10–34) Brutus uses the name of Caesar only twice, but the pronouns 'he', 'his' and 'him' recur 20 times. Brutus seems to find it easier to avoid Caesar's name in order to distance himself from the man whose close friend he has become. As he reads the letter (lines 46–58) Brutus echoes words and phrases: 'Brutus, thou sleep'st. Awake!', 'Speak, strike, redress!' As he does so, the ideas become clearer to him, and he feels more able to assert himself. 'Rome' occurs six times, revealing Brutus' sense of honour as a Roman, and also showing that Cassius has perceptively left the question about Rome incomplete, so that Brutus will feel obliged to 'piece it out'. The actor playing Brutus will be able to gradually build an increasingly clear response to the letter's hints, culminating in his powerful vow: 'O Rome, I make thee promise . . .'. The repetition of 'then' in the last three lines of the extract suggests that Brutus is projecting himself forward in his imagination, to a point in time beyond the present.

Paragraph 8: Lists

Shakespeare often uses lists, piling item on item to intensify and expand different effects, but such itemised lists do not feature significantly in this extract. Rather, there are sequences of effects: 'It is the bright day that brings forth the adder / And that craves wary walking.' The climber faces the ladder as he climbs, 'attains the upmost round' and then 'turns his back' on the ladder, 'Looks in the clouds' and disregards the lower rungs. The 'serpent's egg' will hatch and then will 'as his kind grow mischievous'. These sequences produce a flow of indisputable logic, which convinces Brutus that general tendencies are more reliable than his own personal knowledge of Caesar. The letter Brutus reads lists three courses of action: 'Speak, strike, redress!' These are strongly contrasted imperatives, moving abruptly from the use of argument, through physical aggression and finally to the restoration of justice.

Paragraph 9: Staging opportunities

The stage directions indicate that the action takes place out of doors and, according to Brutus' third line, in the early hours of the morning. Yet there is also a reminder of domestic realities in the scene, for Lucius is called from inside, and is given tasks in the house. Most modern productions avoid cluttering the stage with trees, as the word 'orchard' might suggest, and this will give Brutus' soliloquy under the imagined starlit sky a poignant quietness in which he can develop his argument. Different actors will exploit different opportunities in dramatising the soliloquy, possibly voicing some of it as an interior monologue, and perhaps delivering 'So Caesar may. / Then lest he may, prevent' as though taking the theatre audience into their confidence. Brutus' solitude is both punctuated and emphasised by the return of Lucius, who is promptly sent away again each time he appears, giving the scene a balance between action and contemplation. The letter which Lucius brings is another intrusion, and as Brutus reads it, the actor can reveal the effect it has upon his character's resolution, sometimes repeating a phrase with incomprehension, or with growing understanding as his sense of duty takes hold of him. The timing of the intrusions into Brutus' privacy is finely shaped, so that just after he has come to a resolution after reading the letter, Lucius returns and the conspirators knock on the gate.

Paragraph 10: Conclusion
The scene is a crucial one, revealing the deep internal conflict between Brutus' idealism and his personal experience of Caesar's moderation in the exercise of his power. It also suggests that despite his assertion that only Caesar's death will prevent him from becoming a tyrant, Brutus' mind is far from settled. As the scene progresses, the pace of the action and the tension increase. The letter and the arrival at the gate of the conspirators put subtle pressure on Brutus. Inexorably, it becomes clear that he is about to be carried forward, less by his own decision than by the gathering forces of the conspiracy. The darkness which envelops the action is broken only by the mention of the small candle which Lucius lights in Brutus' study. That the light is prepared for Brutus and that he does not go to it is significant in suggesting the secrecy and obscure nature of the forces acting on him. The soliloquy is crucial in prompting an audience to make a judgement of Brutus. Central in considering his integrity is his line 'Fashion it thus'. It is an admission that a possibility is being conveniently transformed into a proof. Brutus' soliloquy, then, is an exercise in self-persuasive rhetoric, in which he develops his argument to arrive at a conjecture (what Caesar 'may' do and how he 'may' behave), with likely consequences that are unacceptable.

Writing an essay
As part of your study of *Julius Caesar* you will be asked to write essays, either under examination conditions or for coursework (term papers). Examinations mean that you are under pressure of time, usually having around one hour to prepare and write each essay. Coursework means that you have much longer to think about and produce your essay. But whatever the type of essay, each will require you to develop an argument about a particular aspect of *Julius Caesar*.

The essays you write on *Julius Caesar* require that you set out your thoughts on a particular aspect of the play, using evidence from the text. The people who read your essays (examiners, teachers, lecturers) will have certain expectations for your writing. In each essay, they will expect you to discuss and analyse a particular topic, using evidence from the play to develop an argument in an organised, coherent and persuasive way.

You can write about *Julius Caesar* from different points of view. As pages 96–106 show, you can approach the play from a number of critical perspectives (feminist, political, psychoanalytic, etc.). You can also set the play in its social, literary, political and other contexts. You should write at different levels, moving beyond description to analysis and evaluation. Simply telling the story or describing characters is not as effective as analysing how events or characters embody wider concerns of the play – its themes, issues, preoccupations, or, more simply, what the play is about. In *Julius Caesar*, these wider concerns include crowd behaviour, conspiracy, the danger of tyranny, honour, friendship, betrayal, body and spirit.

How should you answer an examination question or write a coursework essay? The following threefold structure can help you organise your response:

opening paragraph
developing paragraphs
concluding paragraph.

Opening paragraph. Begin with a paragraph identifying just what topic or issue you will focus on. Show that you have understood what the question is about. You probably will have prepared for particular topics. But look closely at the question and identify key words to see what particular aspect it asks you to write about. Adapt your material to answer that question. Examiners do not reward an essay, however well written, if it is not on the question set.

Developing paragraphs. This is the main body of your essay. In it, you develop your argument, point by point, paragraph by paragraph. Use evidence from the play that illuminates the topic or issue, and answers the question set. Each paragraph makes a point of dramatic or thematic significance. Some paragraphs could make points concerned with context or particular critical approaches. The effect of your argument builds up as each paragraph adds to the persuasive quality of your essay. Use brief quotations that support your argument, and show clearly just why they are relevant. Ensure that your essay demonstrates that you are aware that *Julius Caesar* is a play, a drama intended for performance, and therefore open to a wide variety of interpretations and audience responses.

Concluding paragraph. Your final paragraph pulls together your main conclusions. It does not simply repeat what you have written earlier, but summarises concisely how your essay has successfully answered the question.

Example

The following notes show the 'ingredients' of an answer.

> Question: 'But, alas, / Caesar must bleed for it.' (Brutus). How important is blood in *Julius Caesar*?

Opening paragraph

Show that you are aware that the question asks you to show your understanding of the contemplation of the murder, the act of the assassination, the symbolic importance of blood and its associations with guilt, with life and with visual memory. Integrate your tracing of blood in its physical and symbolic dimensions with the developing action of the play. So you could include the following points:

- Shakespeare has shaped the play so that the force of the blood images gradually grows, reaching a climax of both verbal and visual impact in the stabbing of Caesar and in Antony's descriptions of the corpse.
- After Antony's oration, blood seems to drain away from the action of the play, except for the brief return to it with Cassius' death.
- Blood is a recurring idea in the play and its presence is developed through a range of images:
  - It is seen as falling from the sky in dreams.
  - It is imagined flowing in 'fountains' and 'spouts'.
  - It is seen as both alarming and nourishing or 'reviving'.
  - With the murder of Caesar, blood can be made vividly visual on the stage.

- It is seen as a symbol of cleansing, in which the conspirators wash.
- The memorable images of blood reinforce the idea that while Caesar's mortal presence has been vulnerable, his spirit remains powerful.

Developing paragraphs
Now write a paragraph on each of the ways in which blood emerges in the dialogue, the images that are developed from it, how its appearance on the stage is important and what it represents as the play progresses. In the development of your essay, aim to identify how the various forms in which blood emerges as an idea are dramatised, and how this relates to the thematic development in the play. The way in which you organise your material will be important in making clear to your reader the line of exploration or argument you are pursuing. Below is an outline of one way in which the points you make might be organised. Each of the headings below might be thought of as the essential topic of the paragraph.

- **The early establishment of blood as an element in the play**
  Blood is mentioned in the opening scene of the play, as Murellus scolds the plebeians for cheering Caesar's return to Rome 'over Pompey's blood'. Shakespeare is thus introducing three ideas which will recur in the play:
  - Pompey, defeated by Caesar, is recalled emotively by his blood.
  - Caesar's rise to power has been through military conquest, implying the bloody clash of armies.
  - Pompey's statue later runs blood as the murdered Caesar lies at its feet.
- **Brutus and 'blood'**
  As the conspiracy gathers momentum, Brutus intensifies the blood imagery, claiming that 'every drop of blood / That every Roman bears' would be contaminated with dishonour if the conspirators break their commitment. He seems to seek to avoid the spilling of blood generally, and:
  - advises against the killing of Antony because 'Our course will seem too bloody';
  - regrets that the destruction of Caesar's spirit means that 'Caesar must bleed for it';

- acknowledges that 'We all stand up against the spirit of Caesar' and that there is no blood 'in the spirit of men'. He wishes that it were possible to 'come by Caesar's spirit' without attacking his body.

Brutus tells Portia that she is as dear to him as 'the ruddy drops / That visit my sad heart'. After the killing Brutus seems to become fascinated by the actuality of blood, wanting to smear it over his arms and sword. He assures Antony that only their hands have done 'this the bleeding business', not their hearts. In Brutus' death, there is a conspicuous lack of blood imagery. The final words in the play are spoken by Octavius Caesar, whose character seems to lack passion or blood, and it is he who sees Brutus' body too, as bloodless: 'Within my tent his bones tonight shall lie'.

- **Dissection/cutting**

  Portia, to prove her devotion, shows Brutus her 'voluntary wound'. Caesar sends to the augurers, who 'could not find a heart within the [dissected] beast.'

- **Calpurnia's visions and dreams**

  Calpurnia dreams of armies fighting in the clouds, 'Which drizzled blood upon the Capitol'. Caesar describes Calpurnia's dream of his statue:

  > Which like a fountain with an hundred spouts
  > Did run pure blood, and many lusty Romans
  > Came smiling and did bathe their hands in it.

  Decius repeats and expands on the details of the image, but assures Caesar that the blood is 'Reviving', and that there will be a demand 'For tinctures, stains, relics' by 'great men'.

- **Blood and wine – the Christ resonance**

  The educated members of an Elizabethan audience would probably have sensed a link between the wine that Caesar drinks with his murderers on the morning of his assassination and blood. Shortly before being stabbed, Caesar reminds the senators that 'men are flesh and blood, and apprehensive'.

- **Making blood visual**

  The staging of the murder will make substantial and visual the blood that has soaked into the play's language. The play offers many opportunities for this:

  - Blood runs at the base of Pompey's statue.

- Blood will be smeared over the arms of the conspirators as they stand around Caesar's body.
- Antony will find Caesar's blood on his fingers as he grasps the hand of each conspirator.
- Caesar's body will be displayed and Antony will reveal the blood on Caesar's robe.

- **Blood as purification**
  Brutus urges the conspirators to 'Stoop' and to 'bathe [their] hands in Caesar's blood / Up to the elbows'. They should 'besmear' their swords and wave '[their] red weapons o'er [their] heads' as they advertise Rome's new freedom. Cassius joins the ceremony, saying 'Stoop then and wash.'

- **Antony's visions and images of blood – the spirit of Caesar**
  For Antony, the conspirators' swords have been 'made rich / With the most noble blood of all this world', and their hands are 'purpled'. He takes each 'bloody hand' as he names the conspirators, and acknowledges the 'slippery ground' on which his 'credit' stands. He asks Caesar's pardon for 'Shaking the bloody fingers of thy foes', and relates tears to blood and Caesar's wounds to eyes: 'Weeping as fast as they stream forth thy blood'. The conspirators are 'Signed in thy spoil and crimsoned in thy Lethe.' Caesar has become 'thou bleeding piece of earth', his is 'costly blood', his wounds 'like dumb mouths do ope their ruby lips'. Caesar's blood ran like one 'rushing out of doors'.

- **Death of Cassius – the last blood image**
  Titinius sees the setting sun reddened by Cassius' death: 'So in his red blood Cassius' day is set.'

Concluding paragraph
Write several sentences pulling together your conclusions. The following points reflect several conclusions that can be drawn from an exploration of the ways in which blood becomes important in the play and how it generates images.

- *Julius Caesar* is a play in which the conspirators set out to annihilate the spirit of Caesar by killing him. The play presents Caesar's body as ordinarily vulnerable and subject to the frailties of age, but his spirit gathers strength through the latter half of the play.
- The conspirators believed Caesar's blood would make legitimate

their claims as liberators of Rome. Antony transforms Caesar's blood into an instrument for their destruction. The powerful blood imagery makes clear the lasting consequences of the murder.

- Despite Brutus' desire for a clean killing, there is no tidy way to kill Caesar. Blood has seeped into the minds of the characters, has coloured the stage. Its stain has become indelible.

- Shakespeare's *Julius Caesar* clearly reflects the anxiety of the Elizabethans about the increasing infirmity of Queen Elizabeth and the lack of a clearly legitimate heir to the throne in 1599. The staged assassination of Caesar, with all its associated blood images, would probably have presented to some members of an Elizabethan audience a spectacle which would have profoundly shocked them when they drew parallels with the state of the monarchy and the future of the realm of England.

Writing about character

Much critical writing about *Julius Caesar* traditionally focused on characters as if they were living human beings. Today it is not sufficient just to describe their personalities. When you write about characters you will also be expected to show that they are dramatic constructs, part of Shakespeare's stagecraft. They embody the wider concerns of the play, have certain dramatic functions, and are set in a social and political world with particular values and beliefs. They reflect and express issues of significance to Shakespeare's society – and today's.

All that may seem difficult and abstract. But don't feel overwhelmed. Everything you read in this book is written with those principles in mind, and can be a model for your own writing. Of course, you should say what a character seems like to you, but you should also write about how Shakespeare makes him or her part of his overall dramatic design.

Cassius and Brutus

Cassius and Brutus are the leaders of the conspiracy against Caesar, but they are very different characters and have very different motives for coming to the conclusion that Caesar must be assassinated. This contrast in their rationale provides complexity in their relationship and dramatic suspense as the conspiracy develops. While Cassius is moved by resentment of Caesar's greatness and by an undying personal antagonism, Brutus is beset by a deeply troubling conflict between his friendship with Caesar and his Republican idealism, which alerts him to the danger that the triumphant Caesar poses to Rome. Both Plutarch and Shakespeare make it clear that Brutus is deeply committed to the tradition of a Roman Republic. His forebear, Junius Brutus, had established an enduring reputation for having driven the Tarquin king from Rome 400 years earlier. Romans had, since then, been fiercely proud of their Republican system of government. Cassius recognises that for the conspiracy to succeed, it must be ruthless in removing all threats to its later success. Brutus, on the other hand, is concerned to justify every action in terms of his own ethical standards. Cassius' judgement is shrewd and insightful, but his bitterness towards Caesar would never dignify the conspiracy with a motivation above the level of self-interest.

Brutus brings respectability to the conspiracy, but his judgement is flawed and his vision obscured by Utopian assumptions (his belief that people can be persuaded by rational argument and that they are as consistent and trustworthy as he believes himself to be). Of the two characters, Brutus comes across as the more sympathetic, and the profound conflict within him makes him more substantial as a tragic figure. There is, too, a greater range of emotional response in Brutus. He is capable of viewing with compassion and magnanimity the uncontaminated innocence and devotion of his young servant, Lucius, and he is stricken with remorse at Portia's pain on being neglected. It is possible that the intense energy of Cassius and his persuasion of Brutus would have reminded an Elizabethan audience of the anxiety about disaffection in the realm, and of attempts that had been made on the life of Queen Elizabeth.

Caesar

Caesar is the ruler of Rome and its empire. As such, he enjoys considerable popular support and is sustained in power by a system which removes the seeds of dangerous opposition (as it did Flavius and Murellus). Yet he is becoming increasingly beset with physical ailments, and with an awareness of his vulnerability. Increasing age seems to make him more aware of his ordinary human condition, yet he stubbornly pursues the image of what he believes he ought to be. This accounts for his recurrent referral to himself in the third person ('Yet Caesar shall go forth'). Ironically, what Caesar seems to fear most is being seen to be afraid. After confiding in Antony about his mistrust of Cassius, he emphatically declares: 'I rather tell thee what is to be feared / Than what I fear'. The conflict between the image he feels obliged to project and his vulnerable humanity is finely captured in his comment to Antony: 'for always I am Caesar. / Come on my right hand, for this ear is deaf'.

In dramatising the character of Caesar, Shakespeare avoids soliciting sympathy for him or arousing alienation towards him. Indeed, the play does not present any one character with a simple or manifestly approved political position. This neutrality is essential for ensuring that the actions of the conspirators, Antony and the plebeians of Rome remain vigorously debatable for the audience. Caesar represents the kind of despotic power which, for the Elizabethans, had the advantage of stability and the disadvantage of certain forms of repression.

Antony

Antony appears first as the trusted friend of Caesar. His robust good health and energetic social life – remarked on by Caesar and Brutus – sets him apart from the other major characters in the play. In dismissing Caesar's accurate perception of Cassius, he shows his own capacity for judgement of individuals to be naive. After Caesar's death, Antony reveals himself as a deeply grieving friend, and as a careful tactician who is prepared to negotiate with Caesar's killers. He is also a passionate and rousing speaker, who is able to use an occasion and visible objects to focus the attention of the listening crowd as he works up their emotions. There is an element of irresponsibility in his unleashing of mob destructiveness with the self-addressed comment, 'Now let it work. Mischief, thou art afoot, / Take thou what course thou wilt!' Any uncritical view of Antony as the avenging hero is shattered by his conduct as a member of the newly established Triumvirate. He agrees to the planned killing of his nephew, and instructs Lepidus to fetch Caesar's will so that Caesar's legacy to the people of Rome can be reduced and some of the wealth redirected to pay for the war against Brutus and Cassius. His dramatic importance emerges after the murder of Caesar. His funeral oration, with its mixture of genuine grief and deliberate crowd arousal, makes the forum scene the pivot on which the action of the play turns. His words to the plebeians emerge as the high point in the effective use of rhetorical language in the play, and its effect on the crowd presented to Shakespeare's audiences a staging of mob destructiveness that Elizabethans generally feared.

Portia and Calpurnia

Feminist criticism regards Portia and Calpurnia, the only female characters in the play, as reflecting submissive roles for women in Elizabethan society. As wives of Brutus and Caesar respectively, they represent the powerless position of women in a male-dominated society (see page 98). Both plead passionately with their husbands. Portia's protest to Brutus about his neglect of her reflects the orthodox obligations of a husband to his wife accepted in Elizabethan marriage. She succeeds at least in making Brutus aware of her needs as a wife and his duty as a husband. Calpurnia's plea is dramatically more pivotal, for she perceives that if she relieves Caesar of the responsibility for deciding to stay away from the Senate House, he will accede to her desperate appeal. He does so, and thus Calpurnia's insight momentarily halts the inexorable thrust of events towards Caesar's assassination. The dramatic suspense which she provides shows on what a fine edge the action of the play is set, and how dependent upon Caesar's character the success of the conspiracy is. The finely timed intervention of Decius – another character with an insight into Caesar's mind – reverses Calpurnia's success, as he abruptly dismisses her fears as 'foolish'.

The plebeians

The common people of Rome are dramatically important in this play. They are the agents in Antony's scheme to destroy the conspirators. Yet their fickleness, the ease with which they can be manipulated into switching their loyalties, seems to place as serious a question over the ideal of a democratic Republic as it does over the centralisation of political power in a ruling class or a benevolent dictator.

Resources

Books

Jan H Blits, *The End of the Ancient Republic: Shakespeare's Julius Caesar*, Rowan & Littlefield, 1992
An examination of the nature of Caesar's rule. Claims that liberty was surrendered by the Romans rather than being seized by Caesar.

Adrien Bonjour, *The Structure of Julius Caesar*, Liverpool University Press, 1958
Examines the roles of superstition, suicide, sleep, together with hints of the 'Fall'.

John Russell Brown, *Shakespeare's Dramatic Style*, Heinemann, 1970
Contains an essay on *Julius Caesar*, which examines the play's meanings in a theatrical context, and shows how variations of rhythm and pace emerge in the text.

Sigurd Burckhardt, *Shakespearean Meanings*, Princeton University Press, 1968
This volume contains a stimulating essay on *Julius Caesar* ('How Not to Murder Caesar'), which explores the pattern of time in the play and its correspondence with the calendar debate of the sixteenth century, and examines Brutus' view of the assassination.

Maurice Charney, *Shakespeare's Roman Plays*, 1961
Contains a detailed discussion of the function of imagery in *Julius Caesar* and the other Roman plays.

Wolfgang Clemen, *Shakespeare's Dramatic Art*, Methuen, 1972
This extended discussion of *Julius Caesar* examines how Shakespeare sustains continuing momentum in the action.

David Daiches, *Shakespeare: Julius Caesar*, Edward Arnold, 1976
A concise and helpful discussion of the play.

L F Dean (ed.), *Twentieth Century Interpretations of Julius Caesar: A Collection of Critical Essays*, Prentice Hall, 1967
A helpful and refreshing range of discussion which includes essays by Robert B Heilman and Sigurd Burckhardt.

Michael Dobson, 'Accents Yet Unknown: Canonisation and the Claiming of *Julius Caesar*', in Jean Marsden (ed.), *The Appropriation of Shakespeare: Post-Renaissance Reconstruction of the Works and the Myth*, Harvester Wheatsheaf, New York, 1991
Dobson's essay examines the adaptations of *Julius Caesar* by rival political groups in the eighteenth century.

B S Field, *Shakespeare's Julius Caesar: a Production Collection*, Nelson Hall, 1980
Comments by eighteen actors and directors in seven different productions.

R A Foakes, *An Approach to Julius Caesar*, Folger, 1954
Central to this discussion is the relation of language to action in the play.

Harley Granville-Barker, *Prefaces to Shakespeare: Julius Caesar*, Nick Hern, 1993
As a critic, a stage director, and a significant influence on theatre directors who followed him, Granville-Barker examines vigorously the relation of the staging of the play to the demands of the text.

David G Green, *Julius Caesar and its Source*, Salzburg Studies in English Literature, 1979
A careful study of the relationship between the narrative of Plutarch and Shakespeare's play.

Mary Hamer, *William Shakespeare: Julius Caesar*, Northcote House, 1998
A feminist view of the play which links the problems of treachery and betrayal among men with the dissociation of men from women in the social world of the play.

Robert Harding (ed.), *Julius Caesar and the Life of William Shakespeare*, Gawthorn Press, London, 1953
Includes the screenplay for the 1953 film and is amply illustrated with photographs from the film.

Geoffrey Miles, *Shakespeare and the Constant Romans*, Oxford Clarendon, 1996
Final chapters deal with Brutus and Antony.

Robert Miola, *Shakespeare's Rome*, Cambridge University Press, 1983
Includes an absorbing essay, 'Rome Divided', on the importance of place in *Julius Caesar*.

John Ripley, *Julius Caesar on Stage in England and America, 1599–1973*, Cambridge University Press, 1980
A detailed stage history of the play from 1599 to 1973, which examines changes in text, staging arrangements, character portrayals and criticism.

Ernest Schanzer, '*Julius Caesar* as a Problem Play', in L F Dean (ed.), *Twentieth Century Interpretations of Julius Caesar: A Collection of Critical Essays*, Prentice Hall, 1968
Schanzer argues that an audience's view of Caesar will determine the view of the conspiracy. Claims that as Caesar eludes easy judgement, the drama can be termed a 'problem play'.

Steve Sohmer, *Shakespeare's Mystery Play: The Opening of The Globe Theatre, 1599*, Manchester University Press, 1999
A stimulating and provocative assessment of the nature of *Julius Caesar* as a play of its time. Sohmer sees the play both as a play for all time and as 'an occasional play, its text topical and packed with allusions to an historical moment'.

T J B Spencer (ed.), *Shakespeare's Plutarch*, Penguin, 1964
Contains Plutarch's biographies of Julius Caesar, Marcus Brutus and Marcus Antonius, on which Shakespeare drew for his *Julius Caesar*.

Vivian Thomas, *Julius Caesar*, Harvester Wheatsheaf, 1992
Especially helpful for the reappraisal of the critical debates and controversies to which the play has given rise.

Peter Ure (ed.), *Julius Caesar: A Casebook*, Macmillan, 1969
Contains a range of critical extracts from 1599 to the mid-1960s, including important essays by Bradley, G Wilson Knight, L C Knights and J Dover Wilson.

John Wilders, *New Prefaces to Shakespeare*, Blackwell, 1988
This stimulating and helpful collection of prefaces for the BBC TV Shakespeare series includes a clear, concise and readable analysis of *Julius Caesar*, and is designed to highlight the essential issues and conflicts in the play as a preparation for responding to a performance.

Richard Wilson, *William Shakespeare: Julius Caesar*, Penguin, 1992
A stimulating examination of *Julius Caesar*, which considers various kinds of text within the play.

Richard Wilson, *Will Power: Essays on Shakespearean Authority*, Harvester Wheatsheaf, 1993
The essay, '"Is This a Holiday?": Shakespeare's Roman Carnival' reveals parallels between Shakespeare's presentation of Rome in the play and Elizabethan London, focusing especially on the significance of the theatre in Elizabethan society.

Richard Wilson (ed.), *New Casebooks: Julius Caesar*, Palgrave, 2002
A valuable collection of modern criticism from 1983 to 1997. Wilson's 'Introduction' (2002) argues that 'for four centuries *Julius Caesar* has remained central to debates about freedom, power and resistance'. The critical essays in the collection emphasise the contemporary relevance of the play. They make major claims for the prophetic significance of *Julius Caesar*, seeing it variously as highlighting the power of the mass media and global communications, as portraying the consequences of totalitarianism and political terrorism, and as a critique of mass society. Wilson's conclusion is that 'Shakespeare's play about the foundation of the Roman empire has now outlasted the British one that it inaugurated, and it may be this example of defiant intellectual resistance to the myth of world conquest which will prove to be the most liberating message of *Julius Caesar* in the fifth century of its existence'.

Films

Between 1908 and 1979 nine films were made of *Julius Caesar*, four of them for television.

The first outstanding cinema adaptation was the Joseph L Mankiewicz film (1953), with Louis Calhern as Caesar, John Gielgud as Cassius, James Mason as Brutus and Marlon Brando as Antony (available on vid___ ?C, ___). Th_ _ was made very much as a film giving priority to actors. Famous ___ wo ___s ___ora Kerr and Gre__ __so__ __ ___ ___ ___, bu_ ___ ___ir_ is ___ ___ ___a_ce was by Marlon Brand___ __ Antony.

Later films include:

- *Julius Caesar* (1959) directed by Stuart Burge for BBC TV.
- *Julius Caesar* (1970) directed by Stuart Burge, with Charlton Heston as Antony, Jason Robards as Brutus and John Gielgud as Caesar. This Technicolor film has been considered 'plausible' but not inspired. (Available on video.)
- *Julius Caesar* (1979) directed by Herbert Wise, with Richard Pasco as Brutus, Keith Mitchell as Antony and Elizabeth Spriggs as Calpurnia. An early production in the BBC TV Shakespeare series, this film reveals the difficulties of accommodating Shakespeare within the constraints of the TV medium.
- *Julius Caesar* (1994) This 30-minute version is part of the BBC's Animated Tales series.

Audio books

Sound recordings of the play are available in the series by Argo, HarperCollins and Arkangel. A CD recording of the Mercury Theatre production adapted by Orson Welles is available from Pavilion Records.

Julius Caesar on the Web

If you type 'Julius Caesar' into your search engine, it will offer you almost 40,000 items. Because websites are of wildly varying quality, and rapidly disappear or are created, no recommendation can safely be made. But if you have time to browse, you may find much of interest.